Ten Foolish Things
Christians Do
to Stunt Their Growth

10 TEN FOOLISH Things CHRISTIANS Do To STUNT Their GROWTH

With Study Guide

Tom Allen

Christian Publications
Camp Hill, Pennsylvania

Christian Publications
3825 Hartzdale Drive
Camp Hill, PA 17011
www.cpi-horizon.com

Faithful, biblical publishing since 1883

ISBN: 0-87509-674-3
LOC Catalog Card Number: 96-84983

98 99 00 01   5 4 3 2

This book is dedicated to my lovely daughters,

Andrea and *Amanda.*

Thanks for keeping your dad honest
about some of the foolish things that I do.

Other books by Tom Allen

Congregations in Conflict

I Wish You Could Meet My Mom and Dad

Rock 'n Roll, the Bible and the Mind

*Joy Comes in the Mourning (David Johnson
with Tom Allen)*

Table of Contents

Foreword

A young boy was asked to sweep the basement by his mother. He went dutifully down the steps and began his chore. While he was sweeping in a dark corner, a mouse scurried from behind a box. Though startled, he decided to chase it down and kill it with his broom. After a considerable battle, he did just that. Holding the mouse by its tail, he marched triumphantly upstairs to show his mother.

Unbeknownst to the little boy, the pastor had arrived for a visit while he was sweeping. So he burst into the living room and, with wide eyes, dramatized the events of the past few minutes downstairs.

"Mom, this mouse jumped out from the corner, and I swung the broom at him, but that didn't kill him. So I chased him to the other side of the room, and hit him again—but that didn't kill him either! Then . . ." The boy paused as he realized that the pastor was in the room. He quickly changed the ending to his story.

"Then, Mom, the Lord took him home."

This is vintage human nature. We do not want to be accountable for our actions. We will even blame the Lord if it will get us out of a jam. In a similar fashion, it has occurred to me that Christians often muddle their relationships with God, fellow believers and unsaved people by refusing to take responsibility for doing "foolish things." This is one of the reasons for the prevalence of immaturity among so many evangelicals. When we ignore the basic principles of God's Word and try to figure things out on our own, we do foolish things which stunt our growth.

This is a book about the basics of healthy Christianity. I offer no magic prayers or formulas for success. But I firmly believe that we must take a serious look at our daily conduct and become accountable to clear, scriptural teaching. In doing this, we can begin to make the necessary corrections and begin to bud and grow again.

When I told my teenage daughters that I was going to write a book about foolish things Christians do, they assured me that I was the right person for the job. On that encouraging note, I got right to work on this manuscript.

If you feel you have reached an impasse in your walk with the Lord, this book is for you. You can break through that growth barrier and reach for higher levels in your spiritual life. But first, we will need to talk about those "foolish things." I can help you. As my daughters have indicated, I'm well qualified.

Rev. Tom Allen
February 1996

Overcrowded
Nurseries

It is every pastor's dream and every child-care worker's nightmare: an overcrowded nursery.

For the pastor, any "baby boom" is a sign of health, growth and promise. Young families always provide hope for the future in any congregation. The expansion or remodeling of the nursery is the easiest project to get approved at a congregational meeting. To be against such a thing would almost be like banning potluck suppers or picketing the annual Sunday school Christmas program.

But weary nursery workers across the land have an entirely different perspective on this overcrowding. To them, it is not exciting or cute. It is not a bright light shining into the future. Rather, it is increased decibel levels; running out of Pampers, Kleenex and baby wipes; accidentally giving the wrong child to an unsuspecting parent; a level of mayhem that would test anyone's Christian character. And of course, Murphy's Law reveals that the length of the pastor's sermon is directly proportional to the degree of nursery overcrowding on any given Sunday—the larger the crowd of babies, the longer the message!

The "spiritual nursery" of the church presents the same distinct emotions. On the one hand, it is the supreme joy of any church to welcome new babes in Christ into the fellowship. How wonderful to hear their first testimonies, to watch them get baptized and to see them grow! Any congregation that is privileged to be overcrowded in this manner is blessed indeed.

Changing Diapers in Corinth

However, the Apostle Paul reflected on another kind of overcrowded nursery in First Corinthians 3:1-4. This New Testament church was a group of "spiritual babies" who desperately needed to grow up and put away their childish behavior. We read:

> Brothers, I could not address you as spiritual but as worldly—mere infants in Christ. I gave you milk, not solid food, for you were not yet ready for it. Indeed, you are still not ready. You are still worldly. For since there is jealousy and quarreling among you, are

you not worldly? Are you not acting like mere men? For when one says, "I follow Paul," and another, "I follow Apollos," are you not mere men?

The apostle's frustration is very obvious here. He is trying to coax overgrown spiritual infants to "grow up." The church at Corinth knew better. Their immaturity was a direct result of their stubborn refusal to obey the Lord and take the next step in their walk with God. Corinth had developed an "overcrowded nursery" which represented just the opposite of vitality. These were not "new babes in Christ" to rejoice over—they were "old babies" in need of repentance and renewal. They were carnal Christians who needed to get a life—a spiritual life. Consider Paul's evidence to verify his accusation:

First, they were unable to digest "spiritual meat"—unable to get beyond the basics and start to build on what they knew. They still had to be bottle-fed. He says with disapproval in his voice, "You are still not ready for solid food." Gerber's baby food is fine for little ones. But it is not at all appropriate for a *teenager* to be slurping pulverized peas!

Second, they were caught up in jealousy, quarreling and carnality in general. Believers who graduate from the nursery are characterized by a desire to encourage others in their success rather than being threatened by them. The mature Christian understands the futility of fighting with his or her brothers and sisters in the Lord. Spiritual depth is confirmed by how well a disciple of Christ can be distinguished from "mere men." But many in the Corinthian church exhibited envy, bickering and other self-centered behavior to such a degree that there was no way to distinguish the believers from the non-believers.

Third, the infantile state of the church at Corinth was revealed by their allegiance to human leaders. Paul was quick to admit his limitations, along with those of Apollos: "[We are] only servants, through whom you came to believe—as the Lord has assigned to each his task" (1 Corinthians 3:5). One mark of maturity in a believer's life is a full allegiance to Jesus Christ as the only Lord and Master. Along with that comes the tacit realization that every human spiritual leader is fallible and subject to the same weaknesses shared by all human beings.

But the Corinthian believers wanted to start the "Church of Saint Paul" and the "Church of Saint Apollos" on opposite street corners. They seemed to be getting excited at the prospect of the competition and conflict that would ensue between the congregations.

This is the group of people Paul found himself writing to—a church full of spiritual babies. Lots of diapers needed changing and lots of bottles needed warming. The nursery was full to overflowing with underdeveloped but overgrown babies. It was not a pretty picture.

What About Today?

Almost 2,000 years later, it is fashionable for those of us in the family of God to assume that Corinth was an aberration. We pat each other on the back with a smug smile that says, "Thank God those days of blatant immaturity are over! Today's Church has really progressed from those childish days of the early Church."

I wish to challenge this assumption. I believe we are facing an epidemic in the contemporary Church of overcrowded spiritual nurseries—congregations full of believers whose growth is severely stunted. A simple review of the three things Paul cited in Corinth plainly reveals our weakened condition as we approach the twenty-first century:

1. No stomach for solid food

The average evangelical today is unable to receive the solid food of God's Word. Christians want to "gather around them a great number of teachers to say what their itching ears want to hear" (2 Timothy 4:3).

I know of a large church which grew to an average attendance of 6,000 in just twelve years. The congregation grew so fast that it was difficult to keep up with everything that was happening.

The senior pastor, a godly man and a very effective communicator, felt a need to stress the message of God's grace during those early years. But when the pastor began to preach the other

side of the grace coin—responsibility and obedience—nearly one-third of that congregation
(about 2,000 people) began to look for another
church. Why? Because they wanted to continue
being bottle-fed the message of God's grace. They
refused to get down from the highchair, pull up to
the table with a fork and knife and begin to digest
the meat of obligation and submission.

2. Jealousy, quarreling and carnality

We are facing a general outbreak of jealousy,
quarreling and carnality. Many believers harbor
jealousy in their hearts over the success of others
in the church. Soloists and worship teams vie for
more visibility. Parents of prodigals envy those
whose children are walking with God. Staff members resent other staff members who have a better
salary or greater profile.

Across the land, we hear of churches fighting
over the most inconsequential issues. People are
up-in-arms over Bible translations, modes of baptism, minor doctrinal differences and worship
styles ("too many hymns" or "too many choruses"). We argue about Sunday night formats,
the role of women, the color of choir robes and
building plans. The list goes on and on.

I know of one church where a board meeting de-
generated into a brawl. (This is not what Paul
meant by "fight the good fight"!) But the most
common form of abuse among Christians is verbal,
not physical. Many a pastor or elder has left a board
meeting with a sick feeling in the pit of his stomach

because of the personal attacks that permeated the atmosphere.

3. Human heroes

Many Christians today are looking to and depending on human leaders instead of Jesus Himself. We think of this as common to big churches, but it happens in congregations of all sizes. Evangelical leaders can develop a "cult following" that becomes very unhealthy—especially if they fall.

The moral failure of spiritual leaders in recent times is a classic illustration of what happens when believers place their hopes and dreams in mere men. Thousands were devastated as they watched their heroes disintegrate on national television. People lost large sums of money through fraudulent investments. The faith of many Christians was shaken because it was founded on the wrong source. "It is better to take refuge in the LORD than to trust in man" (Psalm 118:8).

We have established the fact that immaturity is rampant in the Church today. But how did we develop this "overcrowded nursery"? What are the reasons for this widespread spiritual immaturity? Why are so many believers living stunted, stagnant lives?

No Pain, No Gain

Spiritual growth accelerates in the crucible of testing. This is a tried and true axiom of Scripture, confirmed over and over in the Bible and everyday life. James, writing to a group of persecuted believers, said: "The testing of your faith develops perseverance. Perseverance must finish its work so that you may be mature and complete, not lacking anything" (James 1:3-4).

Most Christians in North America know very little about the testing of their faith. We orchestrate our lives so that we are able to comfortably spend most of our time around other believers. We avoid ridicule in the workplace and at school by blending in with the crowd. Modern Christians really have no concept at all of what it means to "lay your life on the line" for Jesus—and I certainly include myself in this category.

Simple logic tells us that if suffering and hardship are part of the process of spiritual growth, North American Christians will need to find other ways to mature. We live in a climate of tolerance for just about any kind of religious movement. Granted, a few ministries are boldly challenging our culture and suffering the consequences of those confrontations. But this is by far the exception and not the rule.

This could change quickly. We may once again experience rejection, ridicule and widespread persecution. Some theologians argue for a post-tribulation rapture because they feel that only this intense suffering will purge the Church and make the Bride pure for the coming of the Bridegroom. But at present, evangelicals live in a peaceful environment. Therein lies one of the reasons for our overcrowded nurseries.

Inadequate Teaching

Some Christians are not growing these days because they are not being fed meat from Scripture in the first place. Perhaps their pastor is fearful and unwilling to deliver the whole counsel of God. He might have been stung the last time he took a bold stand. Maybe the shepherd of the flock himself has not been taught the deeper truths of the faith and so the people find it difficult to rise above their spiritual mentor.

It is sad to see eager believers denied the privilege of growing in their Christian life because of weak, inadequate teaching. This is why James tells us, "Not many of you should presume to be teachers, my brothers, because you know that we who teach will be judged more strictly" (James 3:1).

The Foolish Things We Do

Comfortable lives and inadequate teaching are real hindrances, but they fail to explain the present state of many Christians' lives. The greatest reason for the overcrowded spiritual nurseries in evangelical churches boils down to this: We do foolish things which stunt our growth.

The Bible is full of illustrations in this regard. Consider some of the foolish things people did:

• Adam and Eve followed the advice of a "snake in the grass" and lost out on a perfect garden (Genesis 3).

- Cain did not listen to God's warning to control his temper and killed his brother (Genesis 4).

- King David got lazy and let Joab lead his troops into war; his idle hands set the stage for his fall into adultery and murder (2 Samuel 11).

- King Nebuchadnezzar, despite Daniel's warnings, refused to repent of his pride and cruelty; through a bout of insanity, God showed him his foolishness (Daniel 4).

- Peter bragged that he was willing to die for his Lord, then denied Him three times (Matthew 26).

- Ananias and Sapphira sold a piece of property to donate to the church, but held back part of the money for themselves; their pretense at a full commitment was a lie to the Holy Spirit, and they paid dearly for it (Acts 5).

These are just a few examples of "foolish things" people did in the Bible. I want us to turn our attention now to ten foolish things today's Christians do to stunt their growth. But rather than merely lamenting our lack of common sense, we will also discover how we can avoid these pitfalls.

May God grant each of us wisdom to deal with anything that may be prohibiting our steady growth in Christ.

IF YOU DID NOT READ
THE INTRODUCTION,
YOU JUST DID A FOOLISH THING!
GO BACK AND READ IT NOW!

Chapter 1

A
M i l e
Wide
and an
Inch Deep

Before "Lemon Laws" were passed in the United States, you had to be very careful when buying a used car. Slick salesmen became proficient in selling automobiles that were beautiful on the outside but defective on the inside.

One of the tricks in those days was to put sawdust in a transmission that was about to expire or required major repairs. This scheme was good enough for a few weeks' worth of smooth shifting, but eventually the transmission would have to be completely rebuilt or replaced. This gave the salesman just enough time to get through the test drives and sell the car quickly to some unsuspecting customer.

In this way, the car could look charming on the outside and sound efficient on the inside. Only time would reveal that the transmission was not at all what it appeared to be. Like plastic filler used to cover rust spots, it was a quick fix that would inevitably lead the owner to a repair shop.

We live in a society that is obsessed with outward appearance. Beautiful faces pervade television ads beckoning all of us to buy this, wear that or eat these in an attempt to look like the perfect models on parade. We are told that we "never get a second chance to make a first impression." From an early age, we are taught to concentrate on the surface. If the veneer is acceptable, it doesn't matter too much what's on the inside. Similar to used car sales, it's the exterior impression that counts.

Foolish thing #1
Christians ignore the inner life with Christ and focus on outward appearance

---

More born-again Christians than we would like to admit have bought into the value system that says, "Focus on outward appearance." To illustrate this point, imagine with me an average Sunday morning in a typical believer's home. Dad gets up, dresses himself, eats his breakfast and heads for the car. Mom has to dress herself, help the children, fix breakfast and get lunch under-way. (But besides that, she has nothing else on her mind!)

Dad begins to honk the horn: "Let's get to church! Let's get to church!" Mom is perturbed with his impatience but continues to get every-thing ready for the departure. Just as Mom and the kids reach the front door, Dad honks the horn again: "Let's get going!"

In the mad rush of things, little Johnny is wear-ing only one sock and Susie managed to put on socks of different colors. Mom is completely flus-tered as she leaps into the car, and an argument ensues.

"Can't you even be patient on the Lord's day?!" she growls.

"God doesn't want us to be late!" he snaps.

There's a general sense of mayhem until they get about two blocks from the church. Dad mus-ters up his holiest tone of voice and issues this proclamation: "Let us get quiet and happy. We are going to worship the Lord!" Silence dominates the car as they glide into the parking space. As the family approaches the front door, a "gospel greeter" awaits them with a big grin and a ques-tion: "So how's this lovely family doing today?" With saccharine smiles, in unison, they say: "Oh we're fine, just fine."

What's wrong with this picture? Dad's impa-tience has thrown the family into a no-win situ-

ation. They are all angry and frustrated because of
how the morning turned out, but they are walking
into an environment where they cannot express
their true feelings. Dad, Mom and the kids are
forced to fake a smile for the sake of maintaining a
proper exterior. Yet on the inside, where it really
counts, each family member knows that things are
not "fine, just fine."

So we learn how to hypocritically polish the
outside while we are hurting inside. Jesus said:
"You Pharisees clean the outside of the cup and
dish, but inside you are full of greed and wickedness" (Luke 11:39). And the Lord said to Samuel:
"The LORD does not look at the things man looks
at. Man looks at the outward appearance, but the
LORD looks at the heart" (1 Samuel 16:7).

Christianity Inside-Out

If we are going to avoid the foolishness of focus-
ing on outward appearance, we must come to
grips with this truth: The Christian life must be
lived "inside-out." Our emphasis must be on deep-
ening our inner life with Jesus. As we change our
focus, we will note that our outward behavior, too,
will become winsome and worthy of Christ.

So how can we begin to live our lives "inside-
out"? How can we change our perspective after
many years of living "outside-in"?

Renew the Commitment to Kingdom Values

We must confess that we have embraced the

value system of this world. Like nonbelievers at work and school, we have bought into this superficial system of thought. We have become experts at "cleaning the outside of the cup" to look good in the company of other Christians. We have learned how to tell those little white lies to cover up what is really going on in our hearts.

We may go for days, weeks or even months without having a meaningful time of prayer, time spent studying God's Word or a moment dedicated to meditation. Nevertheless we faithfully attend church and sing the hymns and choruses. We smile and shake hands when we must and pretend that Jesus Christ is our first priority. We may even serve as the pastor or in a lay leadership position while maintaining this state of mind. This is the essence of foolish thing #1: ignoring our inner life with Christ while we concentrate on our outward appearance.

I gave an illustration once during a sermon by placing a sponge into a glass bowl of colored water. The audience could clearly see that the liquid was blue. I teased them by asking, "When I compress this sponge, will clear water come out?" They responded in unison, "No!" As I proceeded to twist that sponge, the blue water dribbled into the bowl. "When life puts the squeeze on you and me," I said, "what's really in our hearts will come out."

It is during those times of stress that we reveal the depth of our Christian character, or lack thereof. And if we have not devoted time and attention to our private relationship with the Lord, this deficiency will be exposed. No amount of false piety will cover for us indefinitely. No increase in the length of our public prayers will make us seem more holy. Giving testimonies to fool the audience about our true spiritual condition will eventually fail.

This is precisely how a Christian can become "a mile wide and an inch deep." Imagine a vast piece of farmland in the flat plains of Nebraska after a strong thunderstorm in July. At first glance, that site may appear to be a huge body of water inviting us to swim, drink and be refreshed on a hot summer day. But as we step in, we suddenly realize that though it may look like an ocean of water, it is only one inch deep!

In the same way, we may appear to have taken large steps in our Christian walk. But if we have lived our lives "outside-in," we will be a mere mirage of maturity. When people get close enough to us, they will perceive the illusion: width without depth.

Our very first step out of shallowness will be to admit our hypocrisy. We must confess that we have placed enormous emphasis on outward appearance with very little concern about the inner life with Christ. The admission itself will be good spiritual medicine because we must humble ourselves and take off our masks. As we agree with God about this sin, we can be forgiven, cleansed and restored. Then we can begin to focus on what really matters.

Developing the Inner Life

The old chorus says: "Read your Bible, pray every day and you'll grow, grow, grow." But what I am suggesting here goes beyond this traditional admonition. Daily devotions are very important, but we must surpass that mind-set if we want to live "inside-out."

As the deer pants for streams of water,
  so my soul pants for you, O God.
My soul thirsts for God, for the living God.
  When can I go and meet with God?
    (Psalm 42:1-2)

The psalmist paints a picture we can feel here. We watch the deer as he sprints away from the hunter. Faster and faster he runs. When he feels safe again, he pauses. His heart pounds rapidly. He lifts his nose into the air as his head turns to the left, then to the right. Thirst. Overwhelming thirst. A passion to have a long drink at a cool stream. He listens intently. Which way to the closest brook? There it is! And off the deer prances in the direction of that gurgling sound. At last, what he has longed for—that cool drink.

Psalm 42 uses the deer's longing for water to demonstrate the desire we must have for the Living Water, Jesus Christ. We must be passionate about our need for the Lord, our need to be in His presence, our need for His guidance, our need for His protection. We must be aware that in His presence is fullness of joy. We have to realize that apart from His nearness, life is meaningless.

This should not just be a "bunker mentality" when the going gets tough. It is easier, indeed natural, to earnestly seek after God when surrounded by difficulty. The Lord may use trials to get us started in this pursuit, but this holy desperation must become a way of life whether we are experiencing good days or bad days, exciting moments or boring hours.

We may not feel the need to draw near to God when things are going well for us. But that does not change the fact that we need Him every moment of every day. As we understand this reality and learn to ignore the emotional illusion of independence, we will begin to dwell in the presence of the Lord.

The New Testament counterpart to Psalm 42 can be found in Paul's declaration in Philippians 3:10-11: "I want to know Christ and the power of his resurrection and the fellowship of sharing in his sufferings, becoming like him in his death, and so, somehow, to attain to the resurrection from the dead."

The apostle is saying that he will do whatever it takes to fulfill this one obsession: to know Christ in the deepest way possible. If that means partaking of a measure of His suffering, rejection and ridicule—so be it. If it means literal death for the Savior's sake—so be it. There was no price too great to pay, no mountain too high to climb and no trial too severe to endure for this wonderful goal of knowing Jesus more intimately.

Desiring the Desire

When we first become Christians, no one has to tell us to read the Bible and pray. We can't get enough of those things! But as we continue on our journey, we may begin to notice a waning of desire. At times in my walk with the Lord, I've said: "I just don't feel like that deer panting after the water—I don't have the same intensity to know Christ as Paul expressed." There is no benefit in berating ourselves for this lack of craving a deeper inner life with Jesus. Humbly confessing the absence of spiritual passion is truly the first step to regaining it.

There are times when our best prayer will simply be: "Lord, I want to want You. I desire to have a greater desire for You." When David was repenting for his affair with Bathsheba, he uttered these memorable words: "Restore to me the joy of your salvation and grant me a willing spirit, to sustain me" (Psalm 51:12).

Some things had been on the decline in the king's relationship with his Creator. David recognized the fact that if God could not "restore . . . the joy" and a "willing spirit," he would repeat those sins again. He had allowed his inner life to become shallow, and thus he had become a sitting duck for temptation. Now it was time to rebuild those broken foundations and deepen his fellowship with Jehovah.

"How Are You Being?"

If you asked the average Christian how he was doing in his walk with the Lord, he would stumble around a bit, and then probably begin to talk about what he is "doing" for the Lord. "I serve on this committee at church"; "I witnessed a few weeks ago to a work associate"; "I'm using a new book for my devotions"; or "My wife and I attended a marriage seminar." This is typical "outside-in" reporting.

Perhaps we should be asking, "How are you *being*?" Though it sounds awkward, it goes right to the issue of the inner life intimacy with Christ. It's like saying, "How are you on the inside?"

So let me ask the reader: How are you *being*? How are you on the inside? Is the focus of your spiritual energy to develop that inner life intimacy with Jesus, or have you been satisfied with the maintenance of a suitable outward appearance?

There are no shortcuts to experiencing a deeper affection for the Savior. This cannot be packaged into a set of videos and there are no microwave instructions. No instant brand or CD-ROM format exists. No one else can bring this intimacy with Christ to you. You must earnestly seek this for yourself. You must be willing to set aside time for the development of this inner life. "Blessed are those who hunger and thirst for righteousness, for they will be filled" (Matthew 5:6).

Studying and Being Studied

I am reminded of a farmer who proudly announced to his neighbors that his son was attending Harvard.

"What is he studying?" asked one of the neighbors.

"Well, actually," replied the farmer, "he's not studying anything—they are studying him!"

In the same way, we will not succeed by merely reading and studying the Word of God each day. We must take the time to meditate on it so that Scripture has an opportunity to "read and study us." My Old Testament professor at Asbury College, Dr. Victor Hamilton, said one day in a prayer before class, "Lord, we don't come to Your Word to criticize it; we come to Your Word and it criticizes us!"

The psalmist says this about the Christian who longs for that closer walk with God: "His delight is in the law of the LORD, and on his law he meditates day and night" (Psalm 1:2). This is immediately followed with the illustration of the "tree planted by streams of water" (1:3). It is an appropriate picture, in context, of something that takes time to develop over many years. Trees don't just suddenly happen. Likewise we can never truthfully say that we have suddenly learned how to contemplate eternal truth. In a sense, we are always learning how to practice this fine art.

This is what James meant in his admonition that we should "humbly accept the word planted in you, which can save you" (James 1:21). The King James Version uses the stronger term "engrafted" instead of "planted." It means that we are to embrace God's Word in such a way that it becomes a part of the very fabric of our lives. In time, Scripture is so much a part of us that we cannot remember when it was not there. I would argue that this cannot take place if we only give it a quick five minutes in the morning before we rush off to work. If we are sincere about seeking to build this inner life with the Lord, we must commit the necessary time to the process.

Prayer as Two-Way Conversation

As we desire a more intimate relationship with Jesus, we will not just pray to be heard by God, but also to hear from God. We become so adept at offering our wish list to the Lord that we can begin to think that this is the essence of prayer. But the vital component of listening must be present in all true supplication.

We can treat our Savior much like we do our spouses. We give all the orders and instructions, and then walk away before our partner has a chance to give his or her input. As frustrating as this may be for us, it must be even more disappointing for the Master. He has created us. He knows us better than we know ourselves. Not to wait and listen for His voice is irresponsible and foolish for sure.

Some who are reading this may at this moment be making crazy resolutions about giving two hours a day to God "starting tomorrow." But we must be patient with ourselves. If we have only been giving minutes to Jesus each day, we won't be able to jump to an hour overnight. Getting headed in this direction is the important thing.

There are two extremes here. One is to set strict time limits and carefully watch the clock so that the "quota" can be reached. When the timer goes off, God must be through! The other extreme is to sit back and hope that it will just happen. Peace can be found in the middle. We need to structure a time frame while being flexible for those occasions when we may need to expand or contract those parameters. God really does understand those times when we are taken away from our routines because of an emergency. And we will become sensitive to those special occasions when the Lord wants us all to Himself just a little longer.

"Pray continually" (1 Thessalonians 5:17) must be balanced with "the time of prayer" (Acts 3:1). On the one hand, we should continually be in an attitude of prayer. Brother Lawrence called this "practicing the presence of God." At all times throughout the day we can maintain a steady, two-way conversation with the Lord. On the other hand, it is also vital to set aside a specific time for prayer. This is an opportunity to ignore all other concerns and concentrate on speaking to and hearing from God.

Have you ignored the inner life with Christ and

focused on the outward appearance? It's a foolish thing to do, and it will stunt your growth.

Chapter 2

The

L o n e

Ranger
Syndrome

"Hi-Ho, Silver!" With those words, the secretive Lone Ranger was off on another caper with his famous horse. Often riding into the sunset, this masked marvel became the romantic symbol of independence and strict law enforcement. He didn't need anyone or anything. Self-sufficiency was his creed.

Perhaps the most basic sin of the human race is our demand to be totally independent of everyone and everything. Lucifer could not stand the notion that he had to be subservient to Almighty God. He said with reckless arrogance in his heart:

> I will ascend to heaven;
> I will raise my throne

above the stars of God;
I will sit enthroned on the mount of assembly,
    on the utmost heights of the sacred moun-
        tain.
I will ascend above the tops of the clouds;
    I will make myself like the Most High.
        (Isaiah 14:13-14)

The plan did not work. Lucifer was cast out of heaven with the mere flick of God's finger. He was gone before he could even say another "I will . . ." He became Satan, the archenemy of the Almighty.

Having failed in this attempt, the devil decided he would try the next best thing. Because misery loves company, he tempted the first man and woman with the promise of independence from God. This time his plan worked like a charm.

In Genesis 3:1-7, we have the account of Lucifer's campaign of deception. His opening statement is an attack on the very credibility of God: "Did God *really* say . . . ?" Then he twisted the truth ever so subtly: "You must not eat from *any* tree in the garden?" Eve immediately corrected him by explaining that they had enormous freedom, but there was one tree standing in the middle of the garden which was off limits. "Touch that one, and we're dead!" she said.

Satan moved in for the kill. With mocking tones, he proclaimed, "You will not surely die!" There was a pause, and then the devil offered his version as to why they were forbidden to eat from that one tree. "God knows that when you eat of it your eyes will be opened, and you will be like God, knowing good and evil."

There is that phrase again: "You will be like God." It sounds very similar to "I will make myself like the Most High." Lucifer wanted someone else to do the same reckless thing he did. So he baited the hook, threw out the line, caught both Eve and Adam and reeled them into his boat. The major mistake in both situations was the passion to be independent of God. If they could be like Him, they would not need Him. This quest for independence continues today.

F₀₀L I sH thing #2
Christians try to succeed on their own apart from the Body of Christ

---

The Lone Ranger is back. This time she could be an evangelical Christian carrying her Bible off into the sunset. "It's just Jesus and me," she says to herself. She doesn't need the Church, she doesn't need other Christians and she doesn't need fellowship. I've met people like this just about everywhere I have traveled.

Some of them will say that they don't associate with other Christians because they had a bad experience in a congregation way back when. For awhile they looked for the "perfect church," but were unable to locate one. They decided that the Body of Christ was too battered to be of any assistance to them in their walk with the Lord.

In one town where I pastored, I worked out at an athletic club with a man who became a Lone Ranger Christian. He told me that he had become disillusioned with his church. In this instance, the teaching of the Word started to hit too close to home. When I left that town, he was in his eighth month of truancy from the Body of Christ.

We need to know that Scripture is very clear on the role of the church and the need for every believer to find a place in the Body of Christ. My paraphrase of First Corinthians 12:21 is this: "It would be a foolish thing for the eye to say to the hand, 'I don't need you.' "

Paul talks about the essential camaraderie of the fellowship of believers:

> The body is a unit, though it is made up of many parts; and though all its parts are many, they form one body. So it is with Christ. . . .
>
> But in fact God has arranged the parts in the body, every one of them, just as he wanted them to be. If they were all one part, where would the body be? As it is, there are many parts, but one body. . . .

> You are the body of Christ, and each one of
> you is a part of it. (1 Corinthians 12:12, 18-20,
> 27)

There is simply no room for "Lone Ranger"
theology in this teaching. We were created for fellowship with God and other members of His family. To pretend that it could be otherwise is like
talking about a friend of yours who is just a
hand—no arms, legs, torso or head—just a hand!
Such a person could not exist, and neither can a
believer survive without other Christians.

Despite its flaws, we still need the Body of
Christ. We must come to terms with the false notion of the "perfect church"—that congregation is
imaginary. It does not reside in this world. Imper-
fect, fallen men and women are leading the
Church, and there will be problems. A day is coming when the Bride of Christ will be "beautifully
dressed for her husband." But this must wait until
the "old order of things has passed away" (Revelation 21:2-4).

I should say it again: It is foolish to try to
make it on our own apart from the Body of
Christ. In Hebrews 10:25, the writer says: "Let
us not give up meeting together, as some are in
the habit of doing, but let us encourage one another—and all the more as you see the Day ap-
proaching."

Let me suggest three reasons why we need to
be a part of the Body of Christ.

1. Encouragement

According to the verse cited above, encouraging
one another was to be a key function of the
Church. Everyone needs to be strengthened in
this way. No one can go without this ministry indefinitely. There is nothing quite like a smiling
brother or sister coming our way to say: "I love
you and I thank God for your life. You have been
a blessing to me."

Some argue that their church does not exercise
this grace of encouragement. I challenge anyone
who says that with this idea—appoint yourself as
a committee of one to get things started by being
an encourager! This is a two-way street. We have
a need to be uplifted and we have a responsibility
to uplift others. There are embittered Christians
who would be transformed if someone would
come alongside them with a word of encouragement. This ministry is contagious, so let's start an
epidemic!

This is so crucial because we won't find much
encouragement in the world around us. Many believers work in dreary settings where the bottom
line is production, not people. The boss doesn't
care about employee relations as long as the job
gets done. Even when workers go that extra mile
for the company, they often get a glance that says,
"It's about time you earned your pay!"

Many of our friends at church are not receiving
encouragement at home either. In the place where
they should feel the most love and acceptance,

they often experience rejection and ridicule. These Christians come to church longing for that friendly glance, that hug, that sense of reassurance that they do not get at home. This is especially true among single parents, widows and widowers and those who have an unsaved spouse. We must provide a safe haven for these lonely, hurting, precious souls.

The Lone Ranger Christian will miss out on this tremendous blessing. His or her growth in grace will be stunted by this lack of encouragement.

2. Fellowship

Acts 2:42 tells us about the early church, "They devoted themselves to the apostles' teaching and to the fellowship, to the breaking of bread and to prayer."

When I was eleven years old, our family went to Toccoa Falls, Georgia, to attend a camp meeting where my father was the evening speaker. Throughout the week, the adults and the children were separated. We children had our own meetings and programs while the adults had their own separate schedules. Late into the week, I crossed paths with my dad and he asked me how things were going. I inadvertently created a new word with my response. I said, "Dad, camp is great, but I can't wait to get back home and have some more of that good ole familyship!"

Fellowship within the Body of Christ should be "familyship." It is the regular gathering of the family of believers around the person of Jesus Christ. Whether in Sunday school, a small group or a worship service, there is something special about the shared experience of life in the Body of Christ.

John writes, "If we walk in the light, as he is in the light, we have fellowship with one another, and the blood of Jesus, his Son, purifies us from all sin" (1 John 1:7).

The basis for our fellowship together in the Lord is our mutual commitment to an obedient Christian life—walking in the light. It is an atmosphere in which one sinner can show another sinner where to find forgiveness and healing. "As iron sharpens iron, so one man sharpens another" (Proverbs 27:17).

Simply "rubbing shoulders" with other Christians can help us grow up spiritually. As we share our victories and defeats, our joys and sorrows, we begin to realize that we are not alone. There is a common thread that weaves its way through all of our lives.

One of Satan's favorite "fiery darts" is isolation. He wants to make us feel completely secluded in our doubts and struggles. He whispers in our ears, "No one else has this problem. You must be a terrible person!" But in the fellowship of believers, we learn, "No temptation has seized you except what is common to man. And God is faithful; he will not let you be tempted beyond what you can bear. But when you are tempted, he will also provide a way out so that you can stand up under it" (1 Corinthians 10:13).

The Lone Ranger Christian can easily become overwhelmed by the enemy at this point. There is no one to turn to during times of difficulty and despair. This is why the isolated Christian is often defeated.

"Church is OK; I just can't stand the people." Granted, some of God's people are opinionated, picky and hard to get along with. Paul still says, "Bear with each other and forgive whatever grievances you may have against one another. Forgive as the Lord forgave you. And over all these virtues put on love, which binds them all together in perfect unity" (Colossians 3:13-14). This is an exhortation to put up with someone else's idiosyncrasies. Why? Because they will need to put up with your multiple quirks and mine too!

The benefits of life in the Body of Christ far outweigh the personality conflicts that inevitably arise. We need the fellowship of the Church.

3. Accountability

"Encourage [exhort] one another daily, as long as it is called Today, so that none of you may be hardened by sin's deceitfulness" (Hebrews 3:13). The word translated "encourage" here in the NIV is perhaps better understood with the KJV use of the term "exhort." The idea is that we are to challenge each other or hold each other accountable. The reason for the ministry of exhortation is so

we won't become "hardened by sin's deceitfulness."

Many of the Lone Ranger Christians I have en-
countered resist this accountability aspect of the
Christian life. They talk about answering only to
God, but this kind of privatization can become the
perfect cover to hide struggles with sin. Certainly
the Lord is very much aware of our spiritual condition at all times. In that sense we are automatically liable for our behavior, but we need that
human dimension to our accountability as well.
Paul struck this balance beautifully in Acts 24:16,
"So I strive always to keep my conscience clear
before God and man."

The apostle was no Lone Ranger, responsible
only to the Lord. He knew that he also had to answer to brothers and sisters in Christ. When Jesus
spoke about the person who was feuding with his
brother, His advice was this: "First go and be reconciled to your brother; then come and offer your
gift" (Matthew 5:24). Our accountability to each
other takes priority over any money or service we
could offer the Lord.

The men's movement known as Promise Keep-
ers is bringing about a healthy renewal of this emphasis on our responsibility to each other in the
Body of Christ. Small accountability groups are being formed in churches all over the United States.
The Apostle Paul's words are being heeded: "Each
of you should look not only to your own interests,
but also to the interests of others" (Philippians 2:4).

By their very nature, women seem to find it easier to talk intimately with other women about their hurts and struggles. But for men, intimate conversation takes a tremendous amount of effort. Many men were taught to keep their feelings inside in order to "be a man." Men appear to grapple more with pride than their female counterparts too. To admit our weaknesses and failures just doesn't seem very "manly."

This is another point at which the laws of God's kingdom and the laws of this world clash in a dramatic way. To be respected in this world, we need to play up our strengths and deny our weaknesses. In the kingdom of God, we play up our weaknesses and deny our strengths. "Therefore I will boast all the more gladly about my weaknesses, so that Christ's power may rest on me. That is why, for Christ's sake, I delight in weaknesses, in insults, in hardships, in persecutions, in difficulties. For when I am weak, then I am strong" (2 Corinthians 12:9-10).

Christians need the encouragement, fellowship and accountability that only the Body of Christ can provide. The Lone Ranger lifestyle is an unwise approach to Christianity that can only lead to defeat and despair.

I urge anyone who has left the Church to go back to the Body of Christ. Perhaps you shouldn't return to the church you once attended. Maybe they did not encourage you or offer fellowship opportunities. But don't assume that all churches will be like that. You can find a new congregation; there is a place in the Body of Christ just for you!

Chapter 3

A

SpL it

Personality

A few years ago, newspaper and TV reports exposed the deep secrets of a pastor who was highly regarded in his home church and throughout the district. He served on the district executive committee. He was known as a fine preacher, a good husband and a loving father. However, this pastor had a dark side which he kept hidden for many years.

After several confusing months of searching for a bank robber, the police showed up at this minister's church and arrested him in connection with several robberies in the area. The pastor had devised some elaborate disguises, enabling him to steal thousands of dollars. He was using the money to feed a sexual addiction with high-priced call girls at $1,000 per encounter.

How could such divergent practices belong to the same person? One set of actions fell in line with the expectations others would have for a respected pastor and Christian father. But the other behaviors were characteristic of a criminal. This minister had completely divided himself into two very different people. The deeds of one persona had nothing at all in common with the other.

In the study of human psychology, we come across the concept of a split personality. This is in reference to an individual who develops an alterego. Many of us had imaginary friends when we were children. The individual with a split personality, however, begins to believe that the imaginary friend is somehow real and very much a part of him. In just this sense, the person develops two personalities—a Dr. Jekyll-and-Mr. Hyde situation.

The Bible talks about the spiritual corollary to this problem. We could refer to it as a "spiritually split" or "double-minded" personality. In reality, of course, this is not an option for the Christian. Jesus stated this rather bluntly in Luke 16:13: "No servant can serve two masters. Either he will hate the one and love the other, or he will be devoted to the one and despise the other."

Furthermore, James offers a warning to those who are attempting to live with a spiritually split personality. "A double-minded man [is] unstable in all he does. . . . You adulterous people, don't you know that friendship with the world is hatred toward God? Anyone who chooses to be a friend of the world becomes an enemy of God" (James 1:8; 4:4).

F₀ₒLISₕ thing #3
Believers fail to integrate Christ into every aspect of their lives

---

Christians who begin to cultivate a split personality are divided along these lines: a secular persona and a spiritual persona.

While existing in the secular persona, the believer looks very much like all the other good neighbors on the street. He is faithful to his wife. He pays his taxes. He's kind to animals (except, perhaps, that pesky cat next door). He helps with community projects. He mows the lawn for an elderly neighbor. He gives to the food shelf for needy families. He provides a "taxi service" for his kids. But this Christian is cautious and incognito in terms of his commitment to Christ. He says nothing that would rock the boat or challenge anyone's beliefs. His attitude is one that says, "Live and let live." He speaks the "unconverted language" and relates to unconverted values. He is extremely careful not to offend anyone with regard to anything—but he won't stand up for his faith in Jesus Christ.

Then there is the spiritual persona. It is exhibited at church on Sundays, during a weeknight Bible study, at Christian social gatherings and any other setting where it is socially acceptable to be labeled "born again." Other believers look at him and say, "He's committed to Christ"; "He's a great Christian"; "His life is a good witness for the Lord."

He knows the language of this group, too. He enjoys a level of comfort when he is with fellow believers. He knows when to pray and how his prayers should sound. He regularly gives money in the offering. He has most of the hymns and choruses memorized. He can quickly find key Scripture verses. He understands that he should periodically give a testimony to demonstrate that he is alive spiritually.

What we have here are two very different personalities going in opposite directions while trying to exist within one person. It is truly a chaotic state, but one in which many Christians find themselves. Though they love the Lord, it seems impossible for them to integrate Christ into every aspect of their lives. They are afraid of what unsaved friends would think or say if they were to meet the spiritual persona. Perhaps the label that is most dreaded by such a person is "Jesus freak." If the secular and spiritual personas were consolidated, this believer could be categorized as a religious fanatic.

Unfortunately, all of us have observed Christians who are so radical about their faith that they actually do more harm than good for the gospel. In fact, some who think they suffer for the faith actually "suffer . . . as a meddler" (1 Peter 4:15). If we break the rules at the office by taking company time to share Christ, we will be ridiculed—but not for the sake of righteousness. Haunting stories in the news tell about fanatical pro-life supporters killing doctors who have performed abortions— and they would say that they do so in God's name. This kind of bizarre behavior does nothing but reduce the credibility of the Christian faith.

The integration of the Lord Jesus into every aspect of our lives does not mean that we will have to pray out loud in the lunchroom. It does not imply that we should visibly carry and read our Bibles for all to see. It does not even suggest that we must witness to every person who crosses our path in a given day.

What, then, does it mean to fuse the secular side of life with the spiritual so that Christ is an integral part of everything we think, say and do? How will we be changed when we assume a single-minded approach to life? What will it take to be able to say with Paul, "For to me, to live is Christ" (Philippians 1:21)? Let's look at this from three angles: thoughts, words and deeds.

The Mind of Christ

"Your attitude should be the same as that of

Christ Jesus" (Philippians 2:5). The integration
of the Savior into everyday life entails the transformation of our minds so that we think the
thoughts of Christ. We can have the very mind
of Christ as we go throughout the day. Secular
thought patterns can be turned into sacred
thought patterns.

Paul indicates that the first step toward this
metamorphosis will take place as we reject the
world's system of thought and seek a spiritual renewal of our thought process.

> Do not conform any longer to the pattern of
> this world, but be transformed by the re-
> newing of your mind. (Romans 12:2)

> Set your minds on things above, not on
> earthly things. (Colossians 3:2)

> You were taught, with regard to your for-
> mer way of life, to put off your old self,
> which is being corrupted by its deceitful de-
> sires; to be made new in the attitude of your
> minds; and to put on the new self, created to
> be like God in true righteousness and holi-
> ness. (Ephesians 4:22-24)

As our minds are cleansed from the pollutants
of the world's way of thinking, we will experience
a renewal of our thought life which will enable us
to embrace the mind of Christ. Then we can see
the world as Jesus sees it. We will care about
things the way He cares about them. We can
know what it is like to walk in our Savior's shoes

and experience things as He does. In this way, the secular and the sacred become unified.

This change in our thought process will not occur overnight. We will feel the pull of other forces—the world, the flesh and the devil. These powers will tantalize us with all kinds of wicked ideas, but we must choose to be "made new in the attitude of [our] minds" and "put on the new self" (Ephesians 4:23-24). This is a deliberate, daily decision we must make. Paul was referring to this conscious acknowledgement of the Master's closeness when he said, "For in him we live and move and have our being" (Acts 17:28).

Christ is life itself to us (in Him we live). Every movement we make on any given day is in the midst of His presence (in Him we move). Our very essence as persons is defined by who Jesus is to us, in us and through us (in Him we have our being).

This is how all of life becomes spiritual through the transformation of the thought process. When our Lord's thoughts become our thoughts, we will think about all of life's situations in the context of God's kingdom. It will be like having a new pair of glasses.

A man is able to go to the office and have pure thoughts about the women around him. He no longer views that setting any differently than he would a service at church on Sunday morning. Gone is the attitude that says, "Well, I'm back in the world now, so I can lust after women just like other men." Christ is there within him throughout the day. The Lord's presence is real. Jesus has taken control of his mind even in that secular setting. All of his life is now sacred.

A woman can find herself in a setting that reminds her of an abuse she suffered many years ago. But this time, rather than reliving the horror and becoming bitter, she is able to rely on the very mind of Christ to take charge in that painful situation. She refuses to retreat to the secular view. The power of Jesus to bring relief is even more real than the terrifying events that took place. Her Christianity is integrated into every aspect of her past, present and future.

The Words of Christ

Another area where Christians may have two conflicting approaches to life is in what we say. James describes the struggle this way: "Out of the same mouth come praise and cursing. My brothers, this should not be. Can both fresh water and salt water flow from the same spring?" (James 3:10-11).

Some believers seem to have developed two distinct vocabularies. One is for church and the Christian community. The other dialect is used everywhere else. It can be quite surprising and embarrassing to walk in on someone like this who was not expecting to see a fellow believer. I've seen some pretty red faces!

I am not only referring to the use of foul language. It may be displayed in the form of lewd humor, sexual innuendos, slanderous conversation, lying or hateful talk. This "second language" is a foolish thing to develop; it is immature and leads to a "spiritually split" personality.

> Do not let any unwholesome talk come out of your mouths, but only what is helpful for building others up according to their needs, that it may benefit those who listen. (Ephesians 4:29)

> Nor should there be obscenity, foolish talk or coarse joking, which are out of place, but rather thanksgiving. (Ephesians 5:4)

> Rid yourselves of . . . filthy language from your lips. (Colossians 3:8)

> But I tell you that men will have to give account on the day of judgment for every careless word they have spoken. For by your words you will be acquitted, and by your words you will be condemned. (Matthew 12:36-37)

Clearly the expectation of God's Word is that we will judge all of our communication on the basis of its spiritual merit. There is no excuse for any Christian to have a "second language" for use in a secular context because we have turned over the control of our tongues to Jesus Christ. When the Lord takes command of our mouths, even our rebukes will be bathed in love and concern for the one being corrected. We learn how to "fight fair" when we are discussing a disagreement with someone. We won't talk one way at home and another way at church. Christ and His will for our verbal communication will preside over every part of our lives.

The Deeds of Christ

> God anointed Jesus of Nazareth with the Holy Spirit and power, and . . . he went around doing good and healing all who were under the power of the devil, because God was with him. (Acts 10:38)

Here is another area of wide discrepancy. Some Christians act one way when they are with nonbelievers, and then behave in a completely different manner when they are among believers. The distinction can be so striking that a split personality is the only fitting explanation.

The pastor/bank robber I referred to earlier is the very essence of a "spiritually split" personality, albeit an extreme example. Though we may not behave in such wildly divergent ways, the danger of a "spiritually split" personality still looms large. It is vital for us to practice a single set of behaviors. Who we are at church should also be who we are at work and vice versa. We must allow the deeds of Christ to be lived out in us on a consistent basis. "Christ in you, the hope of glory" (Colossians 1:27).

One of the things that impressed me the most

about my godly mother and father was the congruity between their public and private lives. As pastor and pastor's wife, husband and wife, Dad and Mom, we could expect the same person to show up in each role. Many children who are raised in Christian homes become disillusioned by the dichotomy between their "Sunday parents" and their "Monday parents."

Thoughts, words and deeds—these are three areas where we can discover whether or not we are living the Christian life with a split personality.

Have you become two different people trying to live within one person? Do you have a clearly defined spiritual persona and another distinct secular persona? This is a foolish thing that Christians do, and it stunts their growth. It is only as we integrate Christ into every aspect of our lives that we will flourish in the Lord.

Chapter 4

BAD Company

Shortly after their conversion at the age of six-teen, twin sisters were asked out on a double date by a couple of guys. The young men wanted to take them to a questionable movie. Though they would not have thought about it twice before giving their lives to Christ, now they had a check in their spirits. They decided to tell the guys that they would let them know later.

As they debated the issue, they decided to call their pastor. After hearing about their predicament, the minister pointed them to Colossians 3:1-3. They read these words:

> Since, then, you have been raised with Christ, set your hearts on things above,

where Christ is seated at the right hand of God. Set your minds on things above, not on earthly things. For you died, and your life is now hidden with Christ in God.

The girls meditated on this passage and soon came up with their answer. So when the two guys called them back for their response, one of the sisters said, "Thanks for the invitation, but we just recently became Christians, and according to Colossians 3:3, we're both dead and we can't come!"

In the humor of this story, there is a profound principle for victorious Christian living. Following Jesus is not a matter of "Do this; don't do that," but of a change of taste so that we become "dead" to the things that once strongly appealed to us. We have a new willingness to align ourselves with those things that will further the cause of Christ in our lives.

FøLiSh *thing* #4
Christians underestimate the power of outside influences on their growth in grace

---

Do not be misled: "Bad company corrupts good character." (1 Corinthians 15:33)

Do not set foot on the path of the wicked

or walk in the way of evil men.
  (Proverbs 4:14)

Do not make friends with a hot-tempered
  man,
  do not associate with one easily angered,
or you may learn his ways
  and get yourself ensnared.
    (Proverbs 22:24-25)

Many believers, especially new babes in Christ, make the mistake alluded to in these verses. They do not realize the power of unholy alliances. They do not sense the reality of the opposing forces which war against their souls. Often inadvertently, they stunt their growth by allowing inappropriate, spiritually subversive influences to set the agenda. Let's consider some of the areas in which this can happen.

Bad Relationships

Blessed is the man
  who does not walk in the counsel of the
    wicked
or stand in the way of sinners
  or sit in the seat of mockers.
    (Psalm 1:1)

The digression indicated in this verse should be noted. The man begins by walking beside a wicked person. Next, he stands and talks to the sinner. Finally, he sits down with the mocker. There is even a change in the approach of the wicked person. Af-

ter he gets his victim's attention and confidence, he
shifts from "sinner" to "mocker."

This can happen to us when we are in the presence of evil individuals. We slowly become drawn
into their way of thinking. Before we know it, we
begin to accept their mockery of spiritual values.
It is such a subtle process that we may not even
see it or feel it happening to us. But eventually the
damage is done, and our growth in grace has been
impeded.

When we first give our lives to Jesus, we may
still have many old friendships from our "B.C." (before Christ) days. This is to be expected. But how
we handle those relationships can make a big difference in our rate of spiritual progress. There are two
extreme reactions, and both are dangerous.

Some people make a clean break, cutting all ties
to their past. This may even include the total ex-
clusion of relatives who are not Christians. They
get completely immersed in church attendance
and activities and form a whole new set of friends.
They simply choose to forget the old lifestyle and
friends and will have nothing to do with them.

At the other extreme, some believers try to integrate their new faith in Christ with the old lifestyle and friendships. They do their best to
maintain their "past" lives, with the added dimen-
sions of religious fervor and church attendance. It
is mildly annoying to their unsaved friends, but
they will sometimes put up with this new "religion fad" to preserve the relationship.

The problem with the first extreme is that this equates *separation with isolation*. Indeed, many Christians today are so separated from the world that they have become isolated from people who are lost and bound for hell. These believers become cozy in their Christian cocoons. All their friends attend church. They surround themselves with Christian books, Christian television shows and Christian radio programs. They have stacks of Christian videos and sermons on cassette. They have built around themselves a bullet-proof bubble to protect them from every evil influence. In other words, they have become so heavenly minded that they are no earthly good.

This cloistered lifestyle is, of course, completely contrary to our calling as redeemed men and women. We have been commissioned to "go and make disciples of all nations" (Matthew 28:19), and that must begin in our own "Jerusalem," and then move out into the rest of the world (Acts 1:8). This is not an optional agenda for the less timid among us. Each of us has been called to a life that is outwardly focused on those who need the Lord.

> My prayer is not that you take them out of the world but that you protect them from the evil one. They are not of the world, even as I am not of it. Sanctify them by the truth; your word is truth. As you sent me into the world, I have sent them into the world. (John 17:15-18)

Christ casts the vision of an outreach mentality in these terms: "*In* the world, but not *of* it." We can have our boat in the water of this world without allowing the water of this world to flow in and swamp our boat! Separation must never become isolation. We will miss some key steps in the growth continuum if we withdraw completely from the world.

The second extreme will also curtail our progress. We can become so earthly minded that we are no heavenly good. Paul says, "Do not be yoked together with unbelievers. For what do righteousness and wickedness have in common? Or what fellowship can light have with darkness?" (2 Corinthians 6:14).

We can and should establish meaningful relationships with the unsaved while at the same time establishing a clear testimony for the Lord. But often we begin to bond with these people and buy into their value system. The question is, "Will we be people *of* influence, or will we be people who *are* influenced?"

When I attended Appleseed Junior High School, I played on the basketball team. More accurately, I sat on the bench and watched others play. It was a great team, and we went undefeated each season (maybe there was a connection there!). Some of the players on that squad went on to high school teams that advanced all the way to state championship finals in Ohio. Our tall center, Bob, was a friend of mine, even though he was not at all interested in spiritual things. (Bob was 6 feet, 4 inches tall—in the 7th grade!)

Bob heard rumors that I was being harassed by some students for my faith in Christ. (I was called "Reverend Allen" long before I was ordained!) I found out that Bob issued a warning to anyone who ridiculed Tom Allen for being a Christian. I don't know exactly what he told those guys, but I think it involved his switchblade. I was grateful for the fact that my willingness to take a stand for Jesus was respected, even by an unsaved friend. Though I was in Bob's world, he knew that I was not of it. But he appreciated the courage it took for me to stand and be counted.

This is a delicate balance to strike in the Christian life. We want to be an influence without being influenced. We want to be the friend of sinners without embracing their value system. We want to separate ourselves from what worldly people cherish while still cherishing worldly people.

Some of this has to do with timing. A new believer is going to need some space after his conversion. He must have time to grow strong in the Lord before he can face old friends and temptations with courage and conviction. To be thrown back into that arena too soon is a sure formula for failure—he will probably be influenced rather than be an influence.

I advise a newly converted young person to

break up with an unsaved boyfriend or girlfriend if that person does not turn to Christ at the same time. So many have said, "But I want to witness to him." In fact the testimony will get much more respect when that friend sees that Jesus has become the unrivaled first love. And most young people are just not able to grow spiritually while they are emotionally attached to an unbeliever.

There is one very important reason why we should make every attempt not to sever all ties with unsaved friends. After we have been discipled, we are the most likely people to reach those from our past. Someone who has known the power of alcohol will be able to communicate with another person in its grip. A member of the old gang from the neighborhood will have the best chance of touching that gang.

Let me tell you about Ernie. He was a young single man who was part of a small discipleship group in a church I pastored. As I got to know Ernie, he shared with me that he had frequented prostitutes prior to his conversion. I tucked that secret from his past in the back of my mind. After a year of intense training, I challenged this discipleship group to go in pairs to a difficult local mission field. "Get outside of your comfort zone," I implored them. I pulled Ernie aside and said, "I think the two of us should go into the city and witness to the prostitutes!"

Understandably, Ernie hesitated. But I explained to him that the time was right for him to

take this step. I would be with him for the pur-
poses of accountability. Together we would trust
the Lord to use us.

This did not turn out to be a successful venture
in witnessing if the standard was the number of
souls saved. I even heard some new swear words.
But we did get a chance to share Christ, and Ernie
was particularly moved by this experience. He
said to me, "Pastor Tom, for the first time in my
life, I saw these women as something other than
'sex objects'—I saw them as souls for whom
Christ died." He never forgot that journey and,
many years later, Ernie (now married with kids)
continues in his walk with the Lord.

Of course, there will be times when a complete
separation from our past will be unavoidable.
Painful remembrance of extreme hurt and suffering may lead to this. Healing for damaged emotions often requires an ability to deal with the past
and then forget about it as much as possible. Destructive memories will need to be replaced with
constructive ones. Being around the situations and
individuals which caused these hurts cannot be re-
storative. Unsaved friends and relatives may make
this decision for us by simply rejecting us out-
right.

"If it is possible, as far as it depends on you, live
at peace with everyone" (Romans 12:18). The
clear implication of this verse is that it will not always be possible to "live at peace with everyone."
There are some who will just not allow that to

happen. This is especially true in some families where one becomes a Christian and no one else does. This forces other family members to rally around their own religious beliefs even if they aren't sure about them. That new believer will find it very difficult to live at peace with those parents, brothers, sisters and other relatives. But this is part of the cost of discipleship according to our Lord in Matthew 10:37-39:

> Anyone who loves his father or mother more than me is not worthy of me; anyone who loves his son or daughter more than me is not worthy of me; and anyone who does not take his cross and follow me is not worthy of me. Whoever finds his life will lose it, and whoever loses his life for my sake will find it.

Bad relationships can hinder our spiritual growth. We must be sensitive to the Holy Spirit so that we will discover that vital balance—"*in* the world, but not *of* it."

Bad Influences

Never before have Christians been faced with so many diversions coming from so many different angles. It is extremely difficult to cultivate the mind of Christ in a world that has become very noisy with radio, television, videos, computers and compact discs.

When John Wesley went off to college, he

wrote to his godly mother and asked her, "How can I know when something is 'worldly'?" Susannah Wesley wrote back to her young son with great spiritual insight and told him, "Whatever takes away your relish for spiritual things, whatever decreases your passion for the Lord—that thing to you is worldly." This is wonderful advice that is easy to translate into our world today.

Is the music we are listening to "taking away our relish for spiritual things"? Does it "decrease our passion for the Lord"? We will need to look beyond the surface to answer these penetrating questions. Some of what we listen to may overtly lead us away from our biblical standards through lyrics that are blatantly evil. Other forms of music may be more subtly seductive and suggestive of anti-Christ themes and mores. The test devised by Susannah Wesley is challenging to take into the music arena.

How about the television, movies and videos we are viewing? What about the magazines and the books we read? Do our media selections enhance our spiritual growth or detract from it? As we allow the Lord to search our hearts in this matter, He will be faithful to show us any changes that may need to occur.

This is not intended to be an allusion to the infamous "Don't List" of some of our legalistic brothers and sisters. Holiness is not achieved by simply checking off a list of things you "don't do," thereby attaining a deeper level of Christianity. I am simply saying that it is not wise for us to try to grow as Christians while we allow ourselves to be bombarded by all sorts of unscriptural messages through the various media. It's not a matter of saying, "We can't do certain things." Rather, "We don't have to!" Jesus has set us free to seek His heart and follow Him.

It could be argued that some of these materials are "morally neutral," and they would not hurt us or help us. Perhaps the issue with these types of media would center more around the time given to them. It is possible to become so obsessed with sports, table games and other distractions that these things could become spiritually subversive. Though we should make room for leisure and relaxation, we want to make sure that we are not unnecessarily wasting time on things that aren't really important.

Have you underestimated the power of outside influences on your spiritual growth? Are you trapped in bad relationships that are dragging you down in your walk with the Lord? Have you allowed unholy forms of media to invade your thought life and take away your relish for spiritual things? Set yourself free to flourish! Take a long look at what is happening inside your heart. Choose to make some changes and the passion for Jesus will return.

Chapter 5

Diversions

This is a parable of two high school football teams: the Tigers and the Lions. They were preparing to play against each other at the Lions' stadium on its new artificial turf.

During the week before the contest, the Tigers' coach spoke to his players about the astroturf on which they would be playing. He brought in experts to describe how artificial turf was laid down. The coach passed around samples of this carpet so the players could feel it. He talked about the special shoes they would need and how this surface would make a difference when they stopped, started, turned or fell. The coach spent so much time talking about the new surface on which they would be playing that he never got around to discussing a strategy for beating the Lions.

The coach of the Lions, on the other hand, spent the whole week talking about the Tigers. He showed videos from their last three games. He pointed out their strengths and vulnerabilities. He told his team that they could, should and must beat the Tigers. He laid out a clear scheme for defeating them.

Game time finally arrived. The Tigers obviously knew plenty about the surface on which they were playing. They had the right shoes and took all the proper precautions. But those Tigers got convincingly trounced that day for one very simple reason—they failed to keep the main thing the main thing. The Lions were prepared to defeat the Tigers, whereas the Tigers were only prepared to play on the new surface. Though the astroturf discussions were interesting, that was not the most important issue.

F₀ₒLIsH *thing #5*
Believers do not keep the main thing the main thing

One of Satan's greatest diversions is diversion itself. Christians often get completely immersed in "issues," "causes" and "movements." In the process, we stray from the two main things to which every believer is called—knowing Christ and sharing His love with a lost world. Paul said to Titus:

> But avoid foolish controversies and genealogies and arguments and quarrels about the law, because these are unprofitable and useless. Warn a divisive person once, and then warn him a second time. After that, have nothing to do with him. You may be sure that such a man is warped and sinful; he is self-condemned. (Titus 3:9-11)

Again, in Second Timothy 2:16, the apostle states, "Avoid godless chatter, because those who indulge in it will become more and more ungodly."

Throughout these passages, Paul's warning is clear. We must not allow minor matters to cloud the big picture of what God is doing and what God wants us to do. Let me enumerate a few of the diversions the devil is presently using to hinder the work of God's kingdom.

The Organization Diversion

God is pleased with order. "Everything should be done in a fitting and orderly way" (1 Corinthians 14:40). However, taken to an extreme, the intense desire to have everything perfectly organized can become a tragic diversion.

I pastored a church that was situated just a few miles from a nuclear power plant. (Perhaps this ex-

plained the "glow" about the congregation!) Several
key lay people in our congregation were employed
there. I visited a deacon in his office at the plant one
day and was fascinated by what I observed (once I
got past a few layers of security!).

He had me hold two extremely thick notebooks
that were filled with rules, regulations, warnings,
policies, emergency procedures and other items.
They could have been used in a gym as weights
for a bench press! But these elaborate, detailed
materials were absolutely essential in that context.
If guidelines were not carefully followed, tens of
thousands of lives could be jeopardized.

If this mentality is transferred directly to the
governance of the Church, the Body of Christ becomes just another organization as opposed to a
living organism. Church leaders can spend count-
less hours writing and rewriting policies for con-
trolling the staff, for using the buildings and a host
of other matters. Lots of paper can be generated.
Thick notebooks can begin to form.

However, the Church of Jesus Christ can never
be reduced to the same rules and regulations that
would give order and organization to secular insti-
tutions. The Holy Spirit must have complete freedom to work and move as He would choose.
Though we need some guidelines, they must be
kept to a minimum so that Jesus Christ has maxi-
mum autonomy in leading His people.

Recently, a pastor asked me to critique an evan-
gelism strategy which had a heavy emphasis on

prayer. I appreciated many aspects of the approach, especially the accent on breaking down satanic barriers through intense prayer. But I had to point out one glaring fault. The plan incorporated too many committees and subcommittees. I said to him, "By the time everyone has reported to everyone else in this intricate organizational structure, you will all be so worn out that no one will have the time or the energy to actually share Christ with an unsaved person!"

This is the organization diversion. We can be guilty of putting together ornate policy notebooks while lost people march into hell. It is possible to become so enamored with planning outreach that we never really reach out. The main thing must remain the main thing.

The Doctrinal Diversion

My father used a dartboard to describe the varying degrees of importance that should be identified with doctrine. In the middle of the board is the bull's-eye which represents the doctrines worth dying for. These are the essential teachings of the Bible that lead to the kingdom of heaven—the fall of man and our subsequent sinful condition, our inability to be righteous in ourselves, the reality of heaven and hell, the deity of our Lord, the substitutionary death of Christ, the bodily resurrection of Jesus from the dead, salvation in the Savior alone, the verity of His second coming—the "bull's-eye doctrines"

which we must all dogmatically agree upon as
evangelical believers.

The ring around the bull's-eye is not so clearly
defined. There we find doctrines like the rapture of
the Church—pre-tribulation, mid-tribulation and
post-tribulation. Others include modes of baptism,
eternal security, views on the role of women in
ministry and perspectives on the millennium.

As we move concentrically to the outside of the
dartboard, the issues become increasingly more
trivial. We might find items in the outer rings like:

• "Was Paul ever married?"

• "What kind of tree did Adam and Eve partake of
  when they disobeyed God?"

• "Who wrote Hebrews?"

We can begin to see how Satan has used his
classic divide-and-conquer methodology to pro-
mote confusion and conflict among brothers and
sisters in Christ. He has encouraged us to focus on
the outer rings rather than the bull's-eye. Instead
of looking for common ground with regard to the
big picture on which all Christians can and must
agree, we fall into the trap of concentrating on
those insignificant issues on which we disagree.

During a layover at the Atlanta airport one day,
I was reading my Bible. A college student came
over to me and asked if I was a born-again Christian. When I told him that I was, he identified
himself as a student at a very conservative Chris-

tian university. As the conversation progressed, he asked me what denomination I belonged to. I told him that I was an evangelist for The Christian and Missionary Alliance.

He paused for a moment and scratched his head. Then he made a stunning statement I have never forgotten, "Well, I can't say as I've heard about the Alliance, but if there was something wrong with your group, I would certainly know about it!" Here was a young man who was learning to judge other believers by some litmus test that had been devised at his school. He was going through life looking for a fight—searching for any area of disagreement.

Mature Christians realize that they do not have all the answers to some of the tough issues. Some of the greatest theological minds throughout history have grappled with these dogmas and they have not been able to reach a consensus. We can say, "I don't know," without feeling inferior. We can accept the fact that others may have disparate opinions on nonessential doctrinal matters. We can disagree while expressing love and respect for those who see things differently.

My dad used to say with a smile, "Everyone is entitled to his own ridiculous opinion!" or "It's OK if you don't agree with me. When we get to heaven, you'll find out I was right!" or "You may not agree with me, but you still have to love me if you want to get to heaven!"

Obviously there can be no compromise on the

core, "bull's-eye doctrines." Those issues are not debatable. We must embrace truths like this firmly and without apology declare: "This I believe." Aside from those essential creeds, there is room for assorted opinions from godly people who see things in their own unique way. We can waste lots of time and money being occupied with doctrinal issues that have nothing whatsoever to do with the eternal destiny of souls. Truly this is a reckless squandering of the kingdom's resources and values.

The Political Diversion

Many Christians today have become involved in the political process. This is a very important role to assume, and we need the infiltration of dedicated believers into every sector of society. But political involvement can be risky from the standpoint that it can distract us from the main thing. Our twofold mission is to know Christ and to share His love with a lost world. This can certainly be accomplished in the political arena, but our effectiveness will be measured by our prioritization.

For example, many congregations and individual believers have become active in the pro-life movement. Many Christians zealously oppose abortion based on Psalm 139:13-16:

> For you created my inmost being;
>> you knit me together in my mother's
>> womb.
> I praise you because I am fearfully and
>> wonderfully made;

> your works are wonderful,
> I know that full well.
> My frame was not hidden from you
> when I was made in the secret place.
> When I was woven together in the depths of
> the earth,
> your eyes saw my unformed body.
> All the days ordained for me
> were written in your book
> before one of them came to be.

It is hard to read this passage without recognizing the fact that human life begins at the moment of conception. This is truth straight from the heart of the Creator.

Some believers have completely immersed themselves in this issue. The rights of the unborn dominate their time, talents and money. They are so radically devoted to this cause that they have forgotten the importance of reaching those who are "unborn" spiritually.

It could be argued that pro-choice individuals will never commit themselves to the opposite opinion until they have been transformed by Christ. The issue is not so much intellectual as it is moral. If there are no moral absolutes, then a promiscuous man and woman should be able to choose abortion as a solution to their unwanted pregnancy. In that context, human life is not sacred—sexual freedom is exalted. But when a person embraces the Word of God as the standard for a code of ethics, everything changes.

As long as we put our time and energy into the effort to correct people's thinking, it will be wasted time and energy. If we concentrate on changing laws in order to change hearts, we will have gotten ahead of ourselves. The truth of the matter is that sinful human beings will not stop having abortions until Jesus Christ returns to this earth to put an end to these murderous acts.

The same can be said for supporting a Christian candidate during an election. It's wonderful to see believers win a seat in the House of Representatives or the Senate. We should help in their campaigns. But we must bear in mind that we are in enemy territory in this world, and those who are born again will never be in the majority. That was positively guaranteed by the Savior Himself when He said, "Enter through the narrow gate. For wide is the gate and broad is the road that leads to destruction, and many enter through it. But small is the gate and narrow the road that leads to life, and only a few find it" (Matthew 7:13-14).

We can attend the marches. We can become involved in the pro-life movement. We can support Christian political candidates, but we must keep the main thing the main thing. As we share the life-altering truths of the gospel, hearts will be transformed. Only then will minds be changed too.

I have offered three illustrations of some diversions in the church today: organizational, doctrinal

and political. These are just a few of the tactics
that Satan uses to distract us from keeping the
main thing the main thing.

These subtle sidetracks can stunt our growth.
They do so by directing our time, talent and treas-
ure toward causes, issues and movements that do
not further complement our primary agenda.
These items are not at the heart of true discipleship. The less time we give to knowing Christ
and making Him known, the less we will grow in
the Lord.

Paul puts our priority in perspective this way in
Colossians 1:28-29: "We proclaim [Jesus], admon-
ishing and teaching everyone with all wisdom, so
that we may present everyone perfect in Christ.
To this end I labor, struggling with all his energy,
which so powerfully works in me."

Chapter 6

_____

Dead
Sea
Disciples

The Dead Sea is called by that name because it cannot sustain life. The reason for this is very simple—the Jordan River streams into it, but nothing flows out of it. What comes in fresh eventually becomes stale and stagnant. Plants and fish can only survive where there is both inflow and outlet.

All of life is organized around this principle. Our physical bodies must maintain the right balance between eating, digesting and physical exertion. If we just ate all the time and had no way of burning calories or discarding the waste, we would soon get sick and die. A business that is healthy must both take in and give out. Marriage partners must receive and give to maintain a robust relationship. The learning process must have both of these components too.

F*oo* l i*S* h thing
#6
Christians constantly receive with little or no outlet for giving

---

Gerry came to my office when he was twenty-five years old. He was single and had already been very successful as an insurance salesman. He had a nice car and he was purchasing his own home. He had given his life to Christ as a young teen, but he felt that something was missing. He just couldn't pinpoint why he was bored and unhappy as a believer.

I gave Gerry a complete "spiritual." This is like a complete physical, but it deals with all aspects of one's spiritual life. He could not think of any un-confessed sin in his life. Gerry felt that his con-science was clear before the Lord and others. He was having a regular devotional time. He was faithful in giving and church attendance.

Then the Lord prompted me to ask the ques-tion that would point Gerry to the answer. I had overlooked the possibility of spiritual obesity.

"What have you done for someone else lately?" I asked.

He was as stunned by the inquiry as I was startled to be asking it.

"What do you mean by that?" he responded.

"Well, it seems that your life pretty much revolves around you. It appears that you have turned inward, and that may be the reason for your depression," I offered.

We continued to explore this possibility. Was Gerry's feeling that his Christian life was meaningless related to his spiritual obesity? Admittedly, he had become a real porker. He weighed in far too heavy for his height and bone size. He was gobbling up spiritual food but had nowhere to run it off.

Perhaps Gerry had become depressed because he did not have an outlet for the spiritual input he was receiving. Did he need to find a way to get outside of his own little world in order to find happiness? After a lengthy discussion, we decided together that Gerry needed to find an avenue of service in the work of the kingdom. As we did this, Gerry's joy soon returned.

Jesus gave us His personal mission statement in Matthew 20:28. "The Son of Man did not come to be served, but to serve, and to give his life as a ransom for many." This was one of the reasons why Jesus was so joyful. His life was devoted to helping others and meeting their needs. Christ was extremely busy serving others when He was not alone with His Father in prayer. Not much time was left to dwell on His own hurts and burdens.

As a teenager, I would sometimes have bouts of typical adolescent depression. My father had a strange cure that worked every single time. He would take me along to the local nursing home as he ministered to those who were lonely and dying. When I focused on these dear elderly people and their needs, my own troubles just seemed to fade away. This never failed to lift my spirits, and I know I was a blessing to them.

This is one of the casualties of our environment as believers today. It is easy for Christians to become lost in selfish concerns and self-pity. So many born-again people seem to have too much time on their hands, because they are unwilling to offer themselves for the King's service. With few challenges to their faith from the outside, it is natural to turn inward.

Many churches do not have an active outreach ministry. This tends to breed self-absorbed believers who have little or no burden for the unconverted. It is the best possible atmosphere for internal strife in a congregation. Having lost sight of genuine spiritual warfare, these churches begin to clash on some of the trivial matters discussed in chapter 5. There is nothing so frightening as a bored bunch of believers who have lost their focus!

This is happening in many churches. Perhaps you have witnessed this scenario. With no clear vision established for reaching lost people and no goals for growth, the congregation is left to bicker about trivialities. They begin to attack the pastor's pulpit ministry or criticize the version of the Bible being used. Maybe they censure the Sunday school department. The older members begin to complain that they are not being visited. Young families malign the youth program.

Why all the fussing and feuding? The Church has not been challenged to serve the Lord and each other. When Christ's Body is not busy, they tend to become "busybodies." There must be an outlet for the inflow. Disaster is imminent if people do not get out into the battle.

With very few exceptions, I have noticed this trend in my pastoral work—the Christians who seem to struggle frequently with despair are not active in the ministry of the church. And the percentages can be intimidating. Pastors often look at the Sunday morning attendance and shake their heads, wondering why they cannot find enough volunteers to staff various ministries. If each member of Christ's Body would just do a little, every position would be filled and God's people would be more cheerful.

As a general rule, the happiest parishioners are also the busiest! They have learned the secret to a joyful Christian life—give it away. They also realize that as they give they are receiving. "Whoever finds his life will lose it, and whoever loses his life for my sake will find it" (Matthew 10:39).

Satan, the Master of Extremes

If the devil cannot sway us to the far right, he will attempt to pull us to the far left. Chapter 1 talked about the importance of "being before doing," of living the Christian life "inside-out," of having quiet times for prayer (both talking and listening) and meditation. And yet, taken to an extreme, this would lead us to a monk's lifestyle. We could concentrate so much on the inner life with Christ that we never actually live for Jesus out in the world where it counts.

In this sense, chapter 6 is the flip side of chapter 1. We must eventually move out from our intimate relationship with Christ into service for Him that will reflect our intimacy. There is a potential extreme in this line of thinking as well. Many Christians get so busy "doing" things for the Lord that they rarely pause to reflect on their level of tenderness with Jesus.

It matters very little to the enemy of our souls which direction we go in excess. The important thing to Satan is that we move radically one way or the other. This was his original temptation for Eve. Even though she had access to every other tree in that lavish garden, Lucifer convinced her that she needed more. She would never be happy without that one forbidden fruit. We must be aware of this tactic and realize that fulfillment is found in the balance.

The Benefits of Servanthood

Allow me to summarize three benefits of servanthood that I have been alluding to throughout this chapter.

1. Serving keeps us humble.

Jesus used the washing of the disciples' feet to demonstrate this truth in John 13. When He finished, He said this:

> Do you understand what I have done for you? . . . You call me "Teacher" and "Lord," and rightly so, for that is what I am. Now that I, your Lord and Teacher, have washed your feet, you also should wash one another's feet. I have set you an example that you should do as I have done for you. I tell you the truth, no servant is greater than his master, nor is a messenger greater than the one who sent him. Now that you know these things, you will be blessed if you do them. (John 13:12-17)

Washing a guest's feet was customary in New Testament times. The roads were dusty, and it was the proper thing to do. But it was considered "slave's work." So when Jesus got out the water, the basin and the towel, it seemed very strange to His disciples. Peter particularly took offense. "No, . . . you shall never wash my feet!" (13:8). The awkwardness was compounded by the fact that this was not just any man with a towel in his hand. Christ was their Lord and Teacher.

That is precisely why Jesus did this. As their Teacher, He wanted them to understand the importance of humble service. The Savior wanted His leadership to be characterized by "do as I do," not just "do as I say." He could have easily just told them to wash each other's feet as a demonstration of their commitment to serving each other. But Christ washed their feet first as an example.

This had a profound impact on the group. When Peter finally figured out the symbolism, he wanted a complete body wash! Etched in their minds forever would be the Master kneeling before them with His bowl and towel. The disciples would always be reminded of what it means to be truly great.

There is something about the act of waiting on someone else that dissolves our pride. It reminds us that we are no better than anyone else. We are all sinners deserving wrath instead of grace and mercy. Serving others keeps us in a place where we can be used by God—the place of humility. "This is the one I esteem: he who is humble and contrite in spirit, and trembles at my word" (Isaiah 66:2).

2. Serving keeps us dependent.

Peter and John were jailed for "proclaiming in Jesus the resurrection of the dead" according to Acts 4:2. Watch what happens when they are released.

> Peter and John went back to their own people and reported all that the chief priests and elders had said to them. When they heard this, they raised their voices together in prayer to God. "Sovereign Lord," they said, "you made the heaven and the earth and the sea, and everything in them. . . . Now, Lord, consider their threats and enable your servants to speak your word with great boldness." (Acts 4:23-24, 29)

As the early apostles moved to the cutting edge of worldwide evangelization after the Day of Pentecost, they became vulnerable to the attacks of both the Sanhedrin and Satan. It became immediately apparent that some of them would not live long. Others would be tortured and imprisoned. Tribulation lurked around every corner.

The key phrase in the Acts passage above is this: "They raised their voices together in prayer." Serving the Lord pointed them in the direction of complete dependence on the Master. The members of the early church were in way over their heads and they quickly sensed the impossibility of the mission to which they had been called. This is why Paul could say, "I will boast all the more gladly about my weaknesses, so that Christ's power may rest on me. . . . I delight in weaknesses, in insults, in hardships, in persecutions, in difficulties. For when I am weak, then I am strong" (2 Corinthians 12:9-10).

He was strong when he was weak because his frailty forced him to depend totally on the strength of the Savior. The only way he came face-to-face with his weakness was a result of his service. If he had kept his faith to himself, his life would have been easier from every angle. But the fact that he was so radically devoted to Jesus moved him to a place of need and dependence.

Many Christians today do not feel this great need for the Lord's strength because they are not in the midst of service. Hidden away from the pressures of a dedicated servant, they can live a charmed life. They attend church, watch Christian videos and television shows, listen to Christian music and radio stations and enjoy fellowship with Christian friends. They are afraid to venture out into a world of needy people because this would expose their vulnerabilities.

The late Vance Havner wrote a book entitled, *Why Not Just Be Christians?* In it, he describes the lukewarm condition of many believers who have chosen the path of least resistance. Unfortunately for them, "Nothing ventured, nothing gained."

3. Serving keeps us fulfilled.

I mentioned earlier that people who resist serving the Lord are often fearful that their weaknesses will be exhibited for all to see. Though this may be true, there is another side to that coin. Christ becomes our strength in weakness and He is honored when we humble ourselves, step aside and give Him the glory. This is the key to a fulfilling, joyful Christian life. It is rewarding to be "in the thick of it" for Jesus.

> If you suffer as a Christian, do not be ashamed, but praise God that you bear that name. . . . Those who suffer according to God's will should commit themselves to their faithful Creator and continue to do good. (1 Peter 4:16, 19)

The alternative to serving is not a pretty sight. We could refer to it as "sitting and soaking" in the Savior. This is what led Gerry, the man I talked about earlier, to his despondency. He was not a happy, fulfilled Christian. Service was the spark that ignited his heart for the Lord once again.

Imagine a thirteen-year-old boy who got a go-cart for Christmas. He lived on a farm and had many wonderful paths on which to ride. But the boy never actually started the motor and drove it. He was content to just polish it and admire it. We would wonder what was wrong with a boy like that. It's safe to say that he never fully enjoyed his Christmas gift.

The Holy Spirit has given every child of God at least one spiritual gift. We, too, will be happy only when we put those gifts to use in the service of the Lord.

Is your intake much larger than your outlet? Have you found that special place of service that God has arranged for you in advance? The Lord has given you spiritual gifts that must be exercised if you will ever know a sense of completeness in Christ. It is foolish to remain a "Dead Sea disciple."

Chapter 7

ROLLER

COASTER

Religion

The story is told of a man who made an appointment with a Christian Science practitioner. He had a splitting headache and desperately wanted to find relief.

The doctor informed him that the pain was all in his head. The patient declared, "That's right, Doc! It's right across the top of my whole head!"

"No, no, no," the doctor retorted. "I mean you only *think* you have a headache. You must not believe in the reality of pain."

The patient looked a bit confused, and then he said, "Well, then, what am I supposed to do?"

The doctor looked him right in the eye and said, "I want you to go home today and keep repeating to yourself, 'I don't have a headache.' Try this for two days."

For two days, the patient told himself over and over, "I don't have a headache!" But the pain got worse, and he became even more frustrated. He decided he would go back to the doctor.

The Christian Science practitioner told him to go home again, look in the mirror and repeat, "I *really* don't have a headache!"

The patient snapped back, "Well, if it doesn't work, I'll be back to settle my bill! I've got to have relief!"

He tried the advice, but to no avail. He determined he would immediately give this doctor a piece of his mind.

In gentle tones calculated to calm down this irate patient, the doctor said, "I'm sorry that my prescription didn't work for you. It could have if you had really followed my instructions. Here's your bill." He handed the patient a bill for $60.

"Sixty dollars!" exclaimed the outraged patient. But thinking quickly, he reached into his wallet and pretended to pull out three $20 bills. Actually, he did not lay anything on the counter at all.

The doctor demanded, "Hey—where's my money?!"

The patient replied, "Oh, don't worry about it, Doc. Just keep saying to yourself, 'I've got $60, I've got $60, I've got. . . .' "

Praise God, born-again Christians do not subscribe to the philosophy of Christian Science. We do not deny the reality of pain. We believe it is possible to have a bad day, a lousy week, a rough month or a horrible year, but we should not build our lives around our exacting circumstances.

F◯◯Li*SH* thing
#7
Christians live by feelings instead of by faith

We live in a culture that is obsessed with how we feel.

"If you have a headache, take this." "Stomach pain? Take that." "How are you today?" "Are you feeling OK?"

The implication is that if we do not feel good all the time, something must be wrong. There must be a pill, a book or a doctor who can restore those good feelings again! Even though this flies in the face of reality, we tend to buy into this way of thinking.

Christians who don't feel "good" may begin to look within for some secret sin that has brought about their despair. There must be something wrong somewhere. Maybe God is mad at them for some unknown reason. Perhaps they have not had long enough devotions. Could it be because they have not witnessed enough lately?

It may be none of the above. We must be willing to accept the fact that our emotional life is tied

into our humanity. We will have many ups and
downs, some good days and some bad days.
Those fluctuating feelings may have little or nothing to do with our spiritual condition. It is related
to our human condition.

Even though I'm not a kid anymore, I am still a
big fan of amusement parks, especially tall roller
coasters. I rode one in Ohio which started off with
a hill that was 203 feet at its peak. The journey
down that first drop was quite a rush. To enjoy
that kind of trip you must experience both the ups
and the downs. In actuality, you must have both
for the ride to succeed.

The Christian life is not unlike a roller coaster in
this way. There will be high experiences and low
ones, but both are necessary to bring us to maturity
in Christ. Just as I could not expect the feeling of
soaring down that first hill to last indefinitely, we
cannot expect our good days to go on forever.

After the fall of man in Genesis 3, God pro-
nounced this sentence on Eve, Adam and all of us:

> To the woman he said,
>
> "I will greatly increase your pains in child-
>   bearing;
>   with pain you will give birth to chil-
>   dren. . . . "
>
> To Adam he said . . .
>
> "Cursed is the ground because of you;
>   through painful toil you will eat of it

all the days of your life.
It will produce thorns and thistles for you,
    and you will eat the plants of the field.
By the sweat of your brow
    you will eat your food."
        (Genesis 3:16-19)

I don't know what this says to you, but it tells me that because of our fallen human condition, we will have more than just a bad hair day once in awhile. The entrance of sin into our world has introduced all kinds of negative emotions, pain and suffering. This is reality and we must deal with it.

Subject to Feelings, Governed by Faith

Our Lord demonstrated that it is possible to live a life that is subject to feelings but governed by faith.

> Then he got in the boat and his disciples followed him. Without warning, a furious storm came up on the lake, so that the waves swept over the boat. But Jesus was sleeping. The disciples went and woke him, saying, "Lord, save us! We're going to drown!"
>
> He replied, "You of little faith, why are you so afraid?" Then he got up and rebuked the winds and the waves, and it was completely calm.
>
> The men were amazed and asked, "What kind of man is this? Even the winds and waves obey him!" (Matthew 8:23-27)

The disciples were caught in the clutches of a violent cloudburst that threatened to take them under. Jesus, in His humanity, was subject to the feelings of complete exhaustion. It had been a long, draining day of healing and teaching. The rhythms of the waves slowly rocked Him into total relaxation. By the time the disciples anxiously roused Him, Christ was sound asleep.

Though our Lord was subject to feelings, the next part of the story demonstrates how He was governed by faith. He was able to stand on the deck of the ship and command the wind and the sea to become silent. At the sound of the Master's voice, every molecule of water was laid flat like the smooth surface of glass. Subject to feelings, Jesus fell fast asleep. Governed by faith, He could say to the raging storm, "Peace, be still."

In John 11, we have another story that illustrates this truth. The Savior was told about the death of His dear friend, Lazarus, so He traveled to Bethany. When Jesus saw the grieving of Mary and Martha, He was "deeply moved" and "wept." These are natural human emotions when a loved one passes away. The atmosphere of sorrowing relatives is poignant. Our Lord was subject to those profound emotions. But it must be remembered that Christ had said before He left, "Our friend Lazarus has fallen asleep; but I am going there to wake him up" (John 11:11).

Through eyes of faith, the Savior could say that this dead man was merely napping. It would be no problem at all to "wake him up." This was true because He was the One who declared, "I am the resurrection and the life. He who believes in me will live, even though he dies; and whoever lives and believes in me will never die" (John 11:25-26).

His prayer is full of trust in His Father: "Father, I thank you that you have heard me. I knew that you always hear me, but I said this for the benefit of the people standing here, that they may believe that you sent me" (John 11:41-42).

Jesus called for Lazarus to come out of the tomb. We should note that He had to be specific or an avalanche of dead people would have been resurrected! "The rest of you stay dead—Lazarus, you come out!" Then it happened. "The dead man came out, his hands and feet wrapped with strips of linen, and a cloth around his face" (John 11:44). Christ had to give instructions to the stunned audience: "Take off the grave clothes and let him go" (John 11:44).

Subject to feelings, the Redeemer had wept. He cried just like we do at funerals. However, His life was governed by faith. He was able to look into that tomb and command this dead man to come back to life.

So we see from the life of our Master that we should not deny our feelings. These emotions are real and we must not try to cover them up. At the same time, our lives do not revolve around those roller coaster sensations. We can be anchored in our solid faith in our unchanging Lord and Savior.

The Fact, Faith and Feeling Train

Perhaps you remember the "train illustration." A train with three cars is made up of *fact*, *faith* and *feeling*.

• *Fact* represents the locomotive engine.

• *Faith* is the fuel car which feeds the engine.

• *Feeling* is the caboose.

Now it becomes quite clear that the train cannot operate without the first two cars, whereas the caboose is optional. This is a good description of our Christian life—we must place our faith in the facts of God and His Word. He never changes, and Scripture represents a persistent book that does not fluctuate with the times. When all around us is fickle and untrustworthy, the Lord and His Word are eternally dependable.

Feelings, the caboose, can and will come and go. They are not necessary to our fulfillment in Christ. By His grace we will have strong, positive feelings at times during our Christian experience, and we can be grateful for this. But we must never depend on a spiritual high as a measurement for our spiritual depth.

Many movements in evangelical circles today are building an entire doctrinal system around emotional trips. More and more bizarre manifestations are being reported. Surely we need to keep an open mind to the freedom of God's Spirit to work in His own mysterious ways. But we must also be on guard against extortionist appeals to excitable flesh.

The main problem with rallies constructed around highly emotional experiences is that when the thrill of that service is over, that is often the sum and substance of the individual's spiritual depth. His or her joy and testimony are so completely built around those exciting episodes that there may be little left to offer apart from these manifestations. Back on the job in the real world, he or she may live an entirely different lifestyle.

Dr. A.B. Simpson, founder of The Christian and Missionary Alliance, wrote about this in a classic hymn called "Himself":

> Once it was the blessing,
>   Now it is the Lord;
> Once it was the feeling,
>   Now it is His Word;
> Once His gift I wanted,
>   Now the Giver own;
> Once I sought for healing,
>   Now Himself alone.

In this context, we should never forget our Savior's admonition to Thomas: "Blessed are those who have not seen and yet have believed" (John 20:29). The Lord Jesus wants to bring us to a place where we do not depend on feelings to know where we stand with Him. We could paraphrase John 20:29 by saying, "Blessed are those who have not *felt* and yet have believed."

Happiness vs. Joy

Central to this issue is the distinction between happiness and joy. Someone has said that "Happiness is dependent on happenings." Happiness needs a perfect climate with the external circumstances going just right in order to flourish. It resides on the surface and its roots do not go deep.

Joy, on the other hand, is a deeper experience that is not at all dependent on outside events or emotional perceptions. Joy is that profound inner sense of contentment that comes as we walk in the light. Joy is the reward for faithfulness and simple obedience to Christ. It is not quickly realized, but real joy cannot be rapidly swept away either. As we humbly serve the Lord and those around us, we will know genuine joy. Jesus said:

> If you obey my commands, you will remain in my love, just as I have obeyed my Father's commands and remain in his love. I have told you this so that my joy may be in you and that your joy may be complete. My command is this: Love each other as I have loved you. (John 15:10-12)

Is your Christianity based on feelings or faith in the facts of God and His Word? Are you looking for a supercharged emotional experience to verify

the level of your spiritual depth? You need to look
no further than the extent of your daily obedience
to the Lord's will for your life.

When you live by faith instead of living by feelings, you will know the deeper experience of the
joy of the Lord even in the midst of a bad day.

Chapter 8

Bitter
or
Better?

Jim (not his real name) decided to pursue a Master of Divinity degree at one of the leading seminaries in the United States. His wife, Karen (not her real name), agreed to work full time to help him get his education. Both had been raised in Christian homes and attended a fundamental, evangelical church. Their local congregation was just thrilled with the news that this couple was sensing the call of God to enter the ministry. It was a very emotional moment when they left for school that August.

Nothing could have prepared Jim for what happened during his second year in seminary. One day, Karen walked into their apartment and made this simple announcement: "I don't love you any-more and I am leaving you. I will be filing for di-vorce." The word "stunned" would be a very weak description of Jim's reaction to that incredible news.

Now I know what most of my readers are think-ing. *He had neglected her, mistreated her or cheated on her.* Or perhaps you thought, *She was having an affair and just wanted to quickly end the marriage.* You would be wrong with either theory. Jim had been an ex-emplary husband in every way. They had not yet had children, so that stress factor was not a consid-eration. If I have ever known a genuine "innocent party," it was Jim. Karen had simply decided that she was bored and she wanted to find some excite-ment by radically changing her lifestyle.

I will never forget the day that he called me with this tragic story. Jim assured me that he would do everything within his power to restore this marriage for the glory of God. Many agoniz-ing months passed by. His wife began to sleep around with several men. Things were rapidly de-teriorating from bad to worse.

I was speaking at a summer conference about a year after Karen left him, and Jim asked me if he could meet me at the camp. I welcomed him with open arms, and he proceeded to tell me that the divorce would soon be finalized. There was nothing he could do to contest it. I was at a loss for words but I prayed with Jim and comforted him the best that I could.

At this point in the story, one might expect to

hear that Jim lashed out in anger to God and threw away his goal of full-time ministry. But that was not the case. Jim allowed his experience to make him better, not bitter.

His resilience during those heart-wrenching days was remarkable to behold. Jim decided to finish his seminary training after the divorce was granted to Karen. He still had the call of God upon his life even though he had been devastated emotionally through this unbelievable turn of events. Even though he knew that his status as a "divorcee" would limit the number of denominations to which he could apply for pastoral ministry, Jim was willing to trust God for his future.

One year after the divorce was final, the Lord brought a young woman into Jim's life. Carol (not her real name) was a graduate of a Christian liberal arts college. Her husband had denounced his faith to join an eastern religion. His guru told him to leave Carol and he promptly did just that. After a lovely courtship, Jim and Carol were married. Today they have three children, and Jim is flourishing in the pastorate. This is a magnificent illustration of our next item for consideration.

In the world's eyes, Jim—and Carol, for that matter— had every "reason" to be bitter. But Jim realized that when we walk by faith we sometimes have to give up our "reasons."

James offers this advice for facing tough times:

> Consider it pure joy, my brothers, when-
> ever you face trials of many kinds, because

you know that the testing of your faith develops perseverance. Perseverance must finish its work so that you may be mature and
complete, not lacking anything. . . .

Blessed is the man who perseveres under
trial, because when he has stood the test, he
will receive the crown of life that God has
promised to those who love him. (James 1:2-
4, 12)

It is important to note the terms which James
uses. He does not say "*if* you face trials of many
kinds." Rather, he says "whenever." These struggles will come in a variety of shapes and sizes—
"trials of many kinds." The question is not
whether trouble is coming our way—that is an established fact. The real issues are these: How will
we respond under pressure? Will we become "bitter" or "better"?

F*oo*LIS*H* thing
#8
Christians allow
disappointment and tragedy
to make them bitter
rather than better

Some believers are completely shocked to discover that the Lord does not promise His children

a rose garden without the thorns. They assumed that once they had given their lives to Christ, rough places would automatically smooth out for them. In many ways this is true, but we must recognize the balance.

Easier and More Difficult

Living is both easier and more difficult with Jesus in our hearts. He told us, "Take my yoke upon you and learn from me, for I am gentle and humble in heart, and you will find rest for your souls. For my yoke is easy and my burden is light" (Matthew 11:29-30).

Living is easier in that we will have a new sense of joy, purpose and meaning in our lives. Because we know that our sins are forgiven, we no longer have to carry the burden of guilt and shame. Above all, we have found peace with God, and this fact in itself simplifies our lives in so many ways. Nevertheless, it is more difficult in this sense:

> If the world hates you, keep in mind that it hated me first. If you belonged to the world, it would love you as its own. As it is, you do not belong to the world, but I have chosen you out of the world. That is why the world hates you. Remember the words I spoke to you: "No servant is greater than his master." If they persecuted me, they will persecute you also. If they obeyed my teaching, they will obey yours also. . . .

> All this I have told you so that you will
> not go astray. . . .
> In this world you will have trouble. But
> take heart! I have overcome the world. (John
> 15:18-20; 16:1, 33)

There is no escaping the fact that we will have
to cope with many trials because of our association
with Jesus Christ. Christianity is not popular because it shines the light on our sinful condition as
human beings. Our Lord's enemies will become
our own enemies, even if they are members of our
own families.

Other tragedies assail the just and the unjust because we live in a world marred by sin. There is
no use trying to figure out why someone was
killed in the back seat of a car while the other pas-
sengers walked away from the same accident un-
harmed. God was not out to get that individual. It
was just the result of living in a fallen world.

Conformed to the Likeness of His Son

Sometimes we hear one believer say to another
who is going through difficulty, "Don't worry. God
said that all things work together for our good!"
Though the person saying this means well, the one
who is struggling often says to himself, "Yes, but
what could possibly be 'good' about this mess?!"
We must never quote Romans 8:28 without its
complement in verse 29. Consider these verses as a
team: "We know that in all things God works for
the good of those who love him, who have been

called according to his purpose. For those God
foreknew he also predestined to be conformed to
the likeness of his Son, that he might be the first-
born among many brothers" (Romans 8:28-29).

What is the good the apostle is referring to? He
lays that out in verse 29. In all of the situations of
our lives, God is working toward this good purpose: to conform us to the likeness of His Son. We
can become more like Jesus through our afflic-
tions. This is certainly a good thing.

James expressed the same idea with slightly different terminology. He said that the testing of our
faith develops perseverance, and when that goes
full cycle, we will be "mature and complete, not
lacking anything" (James 1:3-4). Maturity can be
equated with our level of Christlikeness.

I still cannot answer all the questions surrounding the breakup of Jim and Karen's marriage—or
Carol and her husband's—from the introduction
of this chapter. But without hesitation, I can tell
you that Jim and Carol were both "conformed to
the likeness of His Son" through the ordeal. Today they are more like Jesus in every way. The
story of this couple continues to touch my heart as
I contemplate their perseverance for the sake of
the gospel.

Jim and Carol would also say that it has turned
out to be a good experience because of what it
taught them about suffering as servants of the
Lord. It was not fun and they would not volunteer
for a second round. Nevertheless God used it in

their lives to make them more like Jesus in His compassion for hurting people.

Bitter or Better?

Think about your own life right now. Have you allowed the troubling times to make you bitter? Are you struggling with feelings of anger and resentment? Do you feel that God has abandoned you in the midst of your difficulty? This is what can occur when bad things happen to immature believers.

On the other hand, these hard times can serve to make you better. You must never fake a smile when going through difficult times as if you do not feel the pain, but you can have the joy of Jesus deep inside when perplexing or strenuous circumstances come your way. You can be confident in God's ability to use each and every situation to make you more like His blessed Son. You can choose to see the light of Jesus at the end of the tunnel. You can say, "Lord, I trust You, even when I cannot trace You."

It is a foolish thing to allow the trials of your Christian life to produce bitterness in your soul. The two rewards for passing these tests have everlasting value: "Perseverance must finish its work so that you may be mature and complete, not lacking anything. . . . Blessed is the man who perseveres under trial, because when he has stood the test, he will receive the crown of life that God has promised to those who love him" (James 1:4, 12).

We can have one reward here and now in this world—maturity (becoming more like Jesus). And we can look forward to another prize in the next world—a crown of life (given to us by Jesus). These guarantees can make the experience of distress more bearable. Bitter or better? The choice is yours.

Chapter 9

The
SIN
That
So Easily
Entangles

Several years ago a DC-10 jet crashed shortly after takeoff. Everyone on board was killed on impact—almost 200 people. Investigators discovered that the right engine had fallen off during the ascent. They found out that one bolt which helped secure the engine housing to the wing was missing. This tiny piece of hardware, costing less than two dollars, was the most probable cause for the crash.

Seemingly small, insignificant items can make a huge difference. This is certainly true about sin. The writer of Hebrews talks about "sin's deceitfulness" (3:13) and "the sin that so easily entangles" us (12:1). God told Cain, "If you do not do what is right, sin is crouching at your door; it desires to have you, but you must master it" (Genesis 4:7).

F₀**o**l**iS**h thing
#9
Christians do not deal quickly and thoroughly with sin

Sin is both aggressive and possessive. Paul employed the analogy of a prisoner to describe the power of the sin nature:

> When I want to do good, evil is right there with me. For in my inner being I delight in God's law; but I see another law at work in the members of my body, waging war against the law of my mind and making me a prisoner of the law of sin at work within my members. What a wretched man I am! Who will rescue me from this body of death? (Romans 7:21-24)

The Romans were very creative when it came to devising new methods to dehumanize and inflict suffering on prisoners. Some who were sentenced to death were tied arm-to-arm and leg-to-leg to a dead body. The prisoner would crawl through the streets begging for someone—

anyone—to cut him free from the rotting corpse. Of course, the person who tried to help the condemned man would be killed also. Eventually the poisons from the dead body would slowly infect the prisoner and he would die an agonizing death.

This is the picture the Apostle Paul used to portray the presence of sin in our lives. It is like that dead corpse tied to us; sin is trying to destroy us. It entangles our lives in every imaginable kind of trouble. Remember the pastor in chapter 3 who was robbing banks in order to support his sexual addiction to pornography and prostitutes? This man had created a baffling, tangled web of deceit and lawlessness. By the time he was finally caught and brought to justice, hundreds of lives had been devastated by his sinful actions.

Most of us do not struggle with evil at this deep level, but we each have the potential for it. No matter how far a person travels down any avenue of sin, it all begins with that first step. If we do not learn how to resolve these issues quickly and thoroughly, we can easily end up farther down that road of sin than we could have imagined. We must learn how to deal with sin and we must never take it lightly.

I'm a Sinner, You're a Sinner

In a culture like ours, it would be presumptuous on my part to assume that all of my readers would admit to being sinners. Even some Christians would find it difficult to be classified in this way.

It sounds so demeaning in a world that announces, "I'm OK, you're OK."

Part of our problem is that we have developed a whole new thesaurus under the heading of sin. We talk about our "faults" and our "idiosyncrasies." We gloss over a bad temper by saying, "It's just 'the German' in me" (or the Italian or the Irish or . . .). Our dark moods are inevitable because we have a "melancholy temperament." Lust is no longer an illicit desire—it is an "addiction."

I contend that we are foolish when we refuse to call sin, sin. The reason is simple. Jesus did not die to forgive us for our faults, our idiosyncrasies, our cultural heritage, our temperament or our addictions. Christ died to cleanse us from our sins. And He can only do this when we refer to sin by its real name.

It is important to understand the basic truth established by the psalmist and Paul:

> All have turned aside,
>   they have together become corrupt;
> there is no one who does good,
>   not even one.
>   (Psalm 14:3)

> All have sinned and fall short of the glory of God. (Romans 3:23)

This is what the Bible says about each and every one of us: "If we claim to be without sin, we deceive ourselves and the truth is not in us" (1 John 1:8). We may dislike this fact, we may choose not to admit it, or we might even attempt to hide it. But no amount of denial will change the reality of our innate sinfulness.

No one had to teach us how to sin. We came "factory equipped" to behave in a sinful manner from our conception. As we watch selfish children fight over toys in the nursery, we understand David's lament: "Surely I was sinful at birth, sinful from the time my mother conceived me" (Psalm 51:5).

Common Sins

In First John 2:15-17, we have a listing of the most basic sins that all of us can relate to:

> Do not love the world or anything in the world. If anyone loves the world, the love of the Father is not in him. For everything in the world—the cravings of sinful man, the lust of his eyes and the boasting of what he has and does—comes not from the Father but from the world. The world and its desires pass away, but the man who does the will of God lives forever.

First, John talks about *materialism*—"the cravings of sinful man." This is the passion to want more than you need. Greedy would be an appropriate synonym here. Solomon said it best. "Whoever loves money never has money enough; whoever loves wealth is never satisfied with his income. This too is meaningless" (Ecclesiastes 5:10).

A friend of mine once put it this way: "If someone makes $50,000 a year, he'll spend $52,000." His point: It does not matter how much a person earns; spending always surpasses that amount. Is there one of us who can say that he or she has not struggled with feelings of envy when looking upon the possessions of another?

The second common sin is *lust*—"the lust of his eyes." This means to passionately desire what cannot lawfully belong to us, and it is most often used with a sexual nuance. Adultery, pre-marital sexual relationships, homosexual relationships and other sensually related sins fit this definition. Again these are familiar areas of temptation for all of us.

Third, John talks about *pride*—"the boasting of what he has and does." Uncle Buddy Robinson, the Nazarene preacher, used to say, "Pride is the only disease known to man that makes everyone sick but the person who has it!" Arrogance is so insidious that we rarely see our own problem with pride. It is so much easier to pick out someone else's boastful mannerisms.

It may be a proud look or an arrogant attitude. Perhaps it is a boastful statement. It would be impossible to count all the angles of conceit. An evangelist friend of mine refers to the five fundamental types of pride:

1. "Pride of Lace" is pride in our clothing.

2. "Pride of Race" refers to racial prejudice.

3. "Pride of Place" is boasting about our position in life.

4. "Pride of Face" is being proud with regard to our outward appearance.

5. "Pride of Grace" is spiritual arrogance—the assumption that we are better Christians than those around us.

We all must deal with pride in one manifestation or another.

Commission and Omission

Another deceptive thing about sin is that it is not just a thing we commit—it may also be something we omit. In other words, sin may be revealed by something we did not do which we should have done. So it is not only what we did—it may be what we did not do.

Sins of commission would be like stealing, swearing or cheating. It is a sin you committed—something you did. A sin of omission would be like failing to visit a sick friend when you knew the Lord wanted you to do it. It is the dereliction of our duty. It is our negligence to respond to situations that require action on our part.

Personal, Private and Public Sins

There are three general categories of sin in

terms of our relationship with ourselves, God and other people. We must be careful to distinguish among these types of iniquity because they must each be handled in a different way.

Personal sin is any sinful act committed against another person. The Bible is clear on how to handle this regardless of the perpetrator: "If your brother sins against you, go and show him his fault, just between the two of you" (Matthew 18:15). In other words, neither party is to announce the offense to other individuals or to a group. Jesus is saying, "Work it out, just the two of you." There is an emphasis on keeping the circle as small as possible while matters are being resolved. It is not scriptural to stand up in a public service and ask someone across the room for forgiveness. We can avoid this embarrassing scenario by following our Lord's clear instructions.

I knew a pastor who was conducting premarital counseling with a young couple. About two weeks before the wedding, they yielded to temptation and engaged in sexual intercourse. They were very repentant and told the pastor about their sin. The minister then made them confess this before the entire congregation, and the church experienced a major split.

I feel quite certain that the pastor was wrong to force this couple into a public confession. This was a personal sin committed between these two individuals and it was not necessary to share it with everyone. Personal transgressions should be confessed personally.

Private sin refers to evil thoughts that have not been put into action. I can remember being in revival services where one person went to another with a shocking revelation: "I want you to forgive me, because I've hated your guts for years!" The other party was totally unaware of those bitter feelings. They had been well disguised behind fake smiles because these emotions were going on internally.

At the end of a week at a youth camp where I was speaking, a young man came to me and said, "Rev. Allen, I want you to forgive me because I have hated you all week." I was gracious in my response to him, but I thought he was out of line. I had no way of knowing how he felt about me. This was a private thing, and it should have been confessed to God alone. Now if he had punched me in the middle of the week and had come at the end of camp to ask forgiveness, I could accept that. However, I am glad that he only hated me in his heart!

Lust, bitterness, envy, jealousy and hatred can each be concealed on the inside where only the Lord can detect it. It can be a private struggle. As long as those thoughts are not acted upon, they need to be acknowledged only before the Savior. Private sin should be confessed privately.

Public sin is any sinful deed carried out in a group setting. At a church board meeting, one member may get angry and say things that are inappropriate in front of the other leaders. For this man to be right with God and fellow board members, he will need to confess his sin in front of that group. The transgression was committed in a public setting and therefore must be reconciled in that same forum. Public sin must be confessed publicly.

Many years ago, my father was relocating his church from one part of town to another. One of his elders was a carpenter by trade, and he was sure he would be consulted for the building project. When it became apparent that he had been overlooked, he began to tell several people about his bitterness. "Can you imagine that construction committee completely shutting me out of this process?!"

Eventually he was convicted by the Holy Spirit for this root of bitterness which had sprung up to trouble many (Hebrews 12:15). Later, he learned that he had been overlooked inadvertently. But because his sin had spread throughout the congregation, he knew that the only way to make it right would be through a public confession. As he did this, many others were convicted of their own bad attitudes in various areas. God used his repentance to perpetuate a mighty revival which continued for several months.

The distinctions between personal, private and public sins can sometimes be subtle. We should pray for discernment so we can deal with each sin appropriately. Great blessing or great shame can come to the Body of Christ according to the way sin is confessed.

Repentance

The concept of repentance has been diluted to the point where it is hardly recognizable in the Church today. This principle was a priority throughout our Lord's ministry, and we must not neglect it as we learn to deal with sin. Jesus said, "Repent, for the kingdom of heaven is near" (Matthew 4:17) and "Unless you repent, you too will all perish" (Luke 13:3).

Repentance was not only presented as a necessity for someone just entering the family of God. Throughout the exhortations of Christ to the churches in Revelation 2 and 3 we find the command to repent over and over again. It is also presented as an essential process in the life of an overcomer. As we truly learn to repent for our evil ways, victory will be ours.

What does repentance mean? Let's consider the answer in three stages.

1. Godly sorrow for sin

Paul said, "Godly sorrow brings repentance that leads to salvation and leaves no regret" (2 Corinthians 7:10). This is not the attitude that says, "I'm sorry I got caught." Rather, it is a sense of deep remorse over the fact that our sins nailed Jesus to the cross. As the words of the song say, "I'm the one to blame. . . . I caused all the pain." We must personalize Christ's work on the cross and realize that it was

my wickedness and your wickedness which drove
the nails into His perfect hands.

2. A change of mind

Although we were going to the left, we now
choose to abruptly stop moving in that direction
and turn 180 degrees to the right. We choose to
forsake evil in all of its forms. We change our
minds about our behavior and about who will be
in charge of our lives.

It is possible to pass through stage one of repentance without making it to stage two. We can have
a temporary emotional episode and for a time feel
godly sorrow about our sinful condition. But we
must move on to a change of mind in order to feel
the full impact of this experience.

3. A change of action

Real repentance involves a change in our behavior. We won't do the things we used to do. We
will have a new "will power"—the dynamic com-
bination of our will with God's power. As we
choose to change our minds, the Lord Jesus will
give us the ability to change our actions.

It is possible to get through stages one and two
only to fail at stage three. We may have godly sorrow and change our minds, but we still may fail to
depend upon the Holy Spirit's power to enable us
to stop our sinful conduct.

This is the essence of true repentance—godly
sorrow, a change of mind and a change of action.

The Spirit's Searchlight

In Psalm 139:23-24, we read, "Search me, O God, and know my heart; test me and know my anxious thoughts. See if there is any offensive way in me, and lead me in the way everlasting." It is easy to read a chapter like this and immediately begin a "witch hunt" for sin in our lives, but we must allow the searchlight of the Holy Spirit to do His work. We are not to go poking around trying to figure it all out. As we seek the Lord, He will faithfully, in His own time, reveal those things that are not pleasing to Him. Some are rather obvious and we can deal with them immediately. Others will be unveiled over time. The important thing to remember is that we must never ignore our sin.

Are you dealing quickly and thoroughly with sin? Are you dealing with both the sins of commission and omission? Are you making the distinction between personal, private and public transgressions? Most importantly, are you learning how to truly repent for your sin? Successful Christians are not believers who never sin; rather, they are the believers who know what to do about sin when it occurs, and they deal with it quickly and thoroughly.

It is foolish to leave sin unattended in your life. This can only lead to greater temptation, more defeat and less growth.

Chapter 10

"I Didn't **KILL** That *ELEPHANT!*"

M y dad always loved the zoo. It was a fun and inexpensive family outing. I'm quite sure the ten children in our family often reminded him of certain residents at the zoo.

When our family lived in Rochester, New York, Dad took us one day to the zoo. As we came to the elephant cage, my father said the animal looked hungry. One could assume that this was always the case with such a massive animal! The sign, which read "Don't feed the animals," had been obscured by foliage. So Dad broke off a small branch from a tree nearby and began to feed the elephant through the bars. The huge mammal enjoyed it immensely, but suddenly it began to choke on the branch.

None of us had ever seen an elephant choke before. Dad assured us that he would be OK and we went on to the other exhibits. On the way out of the zoo later that day, we decided we should check on our elephant friend. As we came to the cage, we were surprised to note that he was still hacking. Dad did a good job of hiding his concern from us, but we later discovered that he was quite worried about this congested animal.

My father did not sleep very well that night. He got up early the next morning and walked outside to get the newspaper. On the sidewalk before him was the front page of the paper with a photo of a dead elephant! He could hardly believe his eyes. Crazy thoughts began to race through his head. *I'm going to have to go to the authorities and confess what I've done! How much will a new elephant cost me? I can just see the headlines: "Rev. Allen Kills Elephant!"*

Dad had temporarily forgotten the old adage, "Read the fine print." When he came to his senses, he studied the article more carefully. Under the photo of the dead elephant was the description of one which died of old age at a zoo in Minneapolis, Minnesota. My father was ecstatic and relieved. "I didn't do it! I didn't kill that elephant!" he exclaimed. He called the local zoo that same day to make sure that "his elephant" was OK. Indeed it was.

In Acts 2:38, Peter said to the audience in Jerusalem, "Repent and be baptized, every one of you, in the name of Jesus Christ for the forgiveness of your sins. And you will receive the gift of the Holy Spirit." The word forgiveness is translated "remission" in some versions. It means "to be discharged from the guilt of." It would be like a jury returning a verdict of "not guilty!" That is the feeling that overwhelmed my father when he realized that he was not looking at the picture of a dead elephant from the zoo in Rochester, New York. He had been "discharged from the guilt of" it—he was not responsible. This illustrates what many Christians struggle with every day of their lives: There is no sense of remitted sins.

F₀ₒₗ isH thing #10
Christians do not accept the unlimited grace and complete forgiveness of the Lord

It is of the utmost importance that I follow chapter 9 with an emphasis on the grace and forgiveness of the Savior. Satan is quick to introduce a cloud of guilt over the heads of unsuspecting believers. The enemy wants us to doubt God's love, grace and unlimited ability to forgive. If we cannot be sure of those things, we will always wonder where we stand with the

Lord, which will keep us from any serious growth in our Christian lives.

This inability to accept the mercy of Christ has a ripple effect in all of our relationships. We are less likely to forgive others who sin against us when our own pardon is in question. Forgiven hearts will find it easier to be forgiving hearts. Jesus implied this in Matthew 6:12, 14-15:

> Forgive us our debts,
>   as we also have forgiven our debtors. . . .
>
> For if you forgive men when they sin against you, your heavenly Father will also forgive you. But if you do not forgive men their sins, your Father will not forgive your sins.

Let's consider several passages of assurance which will enable us to fully accept the unlimited grace and complete forgiveness of Christ.

Who Would Stand a Chance?

> Out of the depths I cry to you, O LORD;
>   O Lord, hear my voice.
> Let your ears be attentive
>   to my cry for mercy.
>
> If you, O LORD, kept a record of sins,
>   O Lord, who could stand?
> But with you there is forgiveness;
>   therefore you are feared.
>
> My souls waits for the Lord

> more than watchmen wait for the morning,
> more than watchmen wait for the morning.
> (Psalm 130:1-4, 6)

This psalm would be on my list of the "top five psalms." The writer has "bottomed out." He was reaching up to touch bottom. In this crisis mode, he begs God to listen to his cry for mercy. Then, in a moment of brutal honesty, this author frankly admits that no one would stand a chance if Jehovah gave us all that we deserved. The record book of our sins would be so heavy that it could not be lifted. We would be crushed under its wicked weight.

As it turns out, forgiveness is God's habit. "With you there is forgiveness." Are these not the words that every sinner longs to hear? What blessed assurance for people like you and me who sometimes do foolish things.

Someone reading this could be saying, "This can't possibly relate to what I have done! I've just piled failure upon failure! There's no way God could be reaching out to me with this kind of hope!" Yes, friend, with the Lord there is forgiveness for even you. It is amazing and incomprehensible, but it is still true.

Some have asked, "How can I accept His forgiveness if I can't understand how He can offer it so fully and freely?" We benefit from the use of electricity every day of our lives, but how many of us understand how it works? I am grateful for the laptop computer on which I am writing this book,

but I could not explain to you the most elemen-
tary facts about the hard drive, the DOS or mega-
bytes. The forgiveness of Christ is not for our
intellectual understanding as much as it is for our
appreciation and enjoyment.

God's Eraser

"I, even I, am he who blots out your transgressions, for my own sake, and remembers your sins
no more" (Isaiah 43:25). In His amazing omnipo-
tence, God has the power to utterly erase the
memory of the sin of which we confess and repent. If we go to Him a second time concerning a
sin we have already confessed, the Lord says, "I
have no idea what you are talking about!" This is
a divine attribute which often puzzles us.

Believers have said to me, "I know that the Lord
has forgotten my past sins, but I can't overlook
them. They continue to haunt me." This is an un-
deniable aspect of our humanity—we do remember our sins. But these memories can serve us in a
positive way. We can choose to remember the past
as a lesson or warning and apply that to present
and future decisions.

The devil would have us recollect the past in a
destructive, morbid manner. He wants to use the
memory of failure against us to create doubts
about our forgiveness and our ability to rise above
temptation the next time. Satan wants to trouble
and torture us with negative, uncertain thoughts
about our relationship with God.

Because of this, we must recall that the guilt of that past sin has been completely cared for on the cross of Jesus Christ. The One who will someday be our judge is the same One who has erased forever the memory of our sins. This is extremely good news as we march inexorably toward that judgment day.

This wonderful verse in Isaiah also underlines the importance of the confession, repentance and forsaking of sin. God can only forget the sin that we forsake. It is vitally important that each sin be placed under the blood of His dear Son so that we can enjoy the benefits of His work on the cross.

East from West

> He does not treat us as our sins deserve
>   or repay us according to our iniquities.
> For as high as the heavens are above the earth,
>   so great is his love for those who fear him;
> as far as the east is from the west,
>   so far has he removed our transgressions
>   from us.
>   (Psalm 103:10-12)

Many of us feel like we never quite get away from the presence of our sins. These transgressions seem to be omnipresent. But the key word here is "feel." Though we may feel that they are near, the facts point in a completely different direction.

The Lord says that our sins have been removed "as far as the east is from the west." There is no point of reference here like New York to California—which was intentional. We can rejoice in the fact that there is an unlimited distance between us and our evil thoughts, words and deeds.

The opposite becomes true for those who try to cover up their sin. "Surely the arm of the LORD is not too short to save, nor his ear too dull to hear. But your iniquities have separated you from your God; your sins have hidden his face from you, so that he will not hear" (Isaiah 59:1-2).

Sin keeps us at a distance from the Lord. We go into hiding and we cannot reach Him. But when we confess our evil ways, everything changes. God's forgiveness then puts sin at a distance from us. So the choice is ours: We can be separated from the Savior or removed from our sins. Let us choose to draw near to Jesus and be estranged from iniquity.

Seven Miles Deep

> Who is a God like you,
>> who pardons sin and forgives the trans-
>>> gression
>> of the remnant of his inheritance?
> You do not stay angry forever
>> but delight to show mercy.
> You will again have compassion on us;
>> you will tread our sins underfoot
>> and hurl all our iniquities into the depths
>>> of the sea.
>>> (Micah 7:18-19)

Micah uses the last few verses of his prophecy to celebrate the breadth of God's mercy toward sinners. Like pardoned criminals, we can be forgiven and restored. Though Jehovah becomes angry with sin, His true delight is to demonstrate mercy and grace. In doing so, the Lord actually crushes our iniquities under His feet. The result is that those sins become unrecognizable and powerless over us.

But there's more. "The depths of the sea" is another word picture used to describe the great lengths to which Jehovah has gone to remove our sin. The ocean is seven miles deep in some places. How wonderful to think that our transgressions have been sunk deep into the murky depths of the ocean floor! Way down there, sin cannot be seen. We cannot hear from our past through the miles of water. There is no way to feel its effect at 35,000 feet below the surface. It becomes as harmless as a caged shark locked away in the dark billows. Truly this is a dramatic way to describe forgiveness.

Not only are we separated from our sins by distance (east from west), but also by substance—thousands of feet of water have come between us and our iniquities. This is a liberating, glorious reality for each of us to claim. Think for a moment about the sin in your past that you regret the very most. Now see it being tossed overboard by the Lord Jesus into the Atlantic Ocean, never to be seen or heard from again. It's gone . . . forever.

Just As If I'd Never Sinned

> All have sinned and fall short of the glory of
> God, and are justified freely by his grace
> through the redemption that came by Christ
> Jesus. (Romans 3:23-24)

Romans 3:23 should be used in isolation only
when trying to prove to someone that everyone is
a sinner. Otherwise, we should always include
verse 24. It's a "bad news, good news" scenario.
The bad news is that we have all fallen short of
God's standard of righteousness through our sinful rebellion. The good news is that we can be
"justified freely by his grace through the redemption that came by Christ Jesus."

Someone has said that a good way to remember
the meaning of "justified" is to break it up into a sentence: "Just-as-if-I'd never sinned." What an incredible concept! The slate has been wiped clean. It's
comparable to a computer hacker who enters the
mainframe system at a police station and wipes out
an entire set of records for a convicted felon. Jesus
cleans our record so thoroughly that no trace of that
sin can be found. It is just as if we had never done it.

Redemption is an Old Testament term that refers
to the release of a slave. One owner could pur-
chase the freedom of someone else's slave. In just
this way, we were "bought back" from the slave
driver Satan when Jesus purchased us with His
own blood. Our justification came by way of this
redemptive act.

Imagine the clean slate we have before the Lord. My father used to take his bright white handkerchief and lay it over his dark black comb. "God doesn't see our sin just like we can't see the comb," he would say. "He only sees the pure righteousness of His Son."

Purified from All Unrighteousness

If we confess our sins, he is faithful and just and will forgive us our sins and purify us from all unrighteousness. (1 John 1:9)

I stressed the importance of that word "if" in the previous chapter. So much depends on our willingness to confess, repent and forsake. Once that is settled, God takes over with His faithfulness and justice to make sure that we are forgiven and purified.

The Lord's faithfulness means that He can be counted on 100 percent of the time. He will always forgive and purify when we confess our sin. We cannot think of a situation where He would not keep this promise. He is faithful.

How can a just God forgive sin? His holy demand for justice was completely satisfied by His Son on the cross. The writer of Hebrews tells us:

The law requires that nearly everything be cleansed with blood, and without the shedding of blood there is no forgiveness. . . . So Christ was sacrificed once to take away the sins of many people. (Hebrews 9:22, 28)

Because Jesus took upon Himself our sins, we

can be forgiven and purified: "God made him who had no sin to be sin for us, so that in him we might become the righteousness of God" (2 Corinthians 5:21).

This remarkable truth initially applies to us when we are born again, and its relevance continues with us throughout our earthly pilgrimage. The Greek here uses the present-continuous tense: "As we continue to confess our sins, He will continue to be faithful and just and He will continue to forgive us our sins, and He will continue to purify us from all unrighteousness."

What an amazing concept—purified from all unrighteousness. A gospel singer in the 1970s used to sing:

> Clean before my Lord I stand,
> And in me, not one blemish does He see;
> When I laid all my burdens down,
> He took them all from me.

Have you confounded the amazing grace of Jesus Christ? We have learned that:

- With God there is forgiveness (Psalm 130).

- God remembers your sins no more (Isaiah 43:25).

- God has separated you from your sins as far as the east is from the west (Psalm 103:12).

- God will hurl your sins to the depths of the sea (Micah 7:19).

- We have been justified freely (Romans 3:24).

- He is faithful and just and will forgive us our sins (1 John 1:9).

These passages apply to any and every sin you may have committed in the past as well as to present struggles with evil. The principles also will pertain to anything that may become a temptation in the future.

As we experience this amazing grace, we can pass it along to others who are filled with shame and remorse. So many struggle with that cloud of guilt hanging constantly over them. We can also more readily forgive those who have hurt us. Knowing of the many times we have been pardoned, we can return the favor to those who have offended us.

It is true that we may have to endure some of the long-term human consequences of our iniquity. King David had to confront the series of tragedies which were set in motion through his wickedness. The individual who is converted in prison will not suddenly be released from his or her jail sentence. Divorced persons may not always be able to be reconciled after they have been forgiven. But the important thing to remember is the unlimited grace and complete forgiveness which is ours for the asking.

In fact, it is silly to reject this amazing grace and full forgiveness of Jesus Christ. It can only lead to a return to the cycle of sin, guilt and defeat.

Choose today to believe what God has said about sin, forgiveness and restoration.

Chapter 11

"*Life*...
to the
FULL"

One of the leaders of my church's boys' club was a man named Arlin. I was just coming into my teenage fascination with automobiles when Arlin showed me his 1957 Plymouth Fury. It had a huge V-8 engine with a double four-barrel. I was not quite sure what that meant except that it used a lot more gas. It was also very fast and powerful—I almost landed in the back seat during my first ride.

This '57 Fury was in original, mint condition. It was stored inside during the winter. White sheets were draped across the seats to keep them in perfect condition. It was truly a thing of beauty. Arlin promised to go with me to buy my first car, and I determined that it would be a car from the '50s era.

I found my first car at a dealership about thirty miles from home. It was a 1958 Chevy—coral (pink) and white, with a little rust thrown in for extra style. Arlin checked it out for me both inside and out. The 283 V-8 was good on gas and had adequate power. He told me that with some body work, I could have a nice car. So I shelled out the $450 and drove it home. With putty, paint and pampering, it began to look great.

Arlin called me one day while I was still fixing up my "new" car. He said, "Tom, would you like to go see a real classic car from the '50s?" It took me all of five seconds to decide and away we went.

We parked in front of an old home on Third Street, went to the front door and rang the door-bell. An elderly lady finally made it to the entranceway and motioned for us to go around to the back of the house. Behind her home was an old garage that looked more like a small-scale barn. Arlin swung open the large doors, and there it sat on the wooden floor of her garage.

It was a 1955 Chevy Bel Aire and it looked brand new. The seats looked like no one had ever sat in them before. The paint job was immaculate without a single visible scratch. The chrome glistened as sunlight began to stream in. Arlin signaled for me to join him as he stared at the odometer. "24,000 original miles, Tom. Not bad for an eighteen-year-old car!"

She was asking $1,100 for the Chevy. Though it was a steal, it was way beyond my means. So I returned to my '58 Chevy that day grateful that I had a vehicle, but cognizant of the fact that I had seen a genuine classic.

About two weeks later, Arlin called me with a shocking piece of news. Shortly after we had looked at this '55 Bel Aire, a father bought it for his teenage daughter. She was partying one Friday night and ended up in a terrible accident. Though no one was seriously hurt, the gorgeous automobile was totaled.

Arlin asked me, "Do you want to go to the funeral?"

"What do you mean?" I asked, puzzled.

He clarified, "Do you want to go to the junkyard where they took that Chevy?"

It seemed like the right thing to do for a couple of old car buffs. He picked me up a few hours later and we traveled down Route 13 to the wrecking yard. After scrounging around for awhile we found the smashed remains of that classic old car. It was hard to believe the damage that could be done through one careless accident. This vehicle went from prized possession to despised debris in a matter of moments.

That trip to the junkyard stuck with me. I've thought of the many Christians I've known through the years who started out with such great promise. Everyone was certain that they would make a great impact for Christ. But because they

were trapped in some of the foolish things I've described in this book, they had a terrible crash. God
had to set them aside in the evangelical junkyard.
Yes, they were forgiven, but the magnitude of
their collision had severely reduced their useful-
ness for kingdom work.

King David was never quite the same after he
had the affair with Bathsheba and had her husband killed in battle. He was not able to be restored to the same level of effectiveness. Because
of the great grace of the Lord, David was still
called "a man after God's own heart." But there is
no denying the fact that David could have been
used in a greater way had he not slept with another man's wife and killed her husband.

We do not have to begin our Christian life with
a bang only to crash and burn later in our walk
with the Lord. This is not the Savior's plan for
even one of His children. God's blueprint for each
of us is to become more and more like Jesus.
Christ put it this way in John 10:10: "I have come
that they may have life, and have it to the full." In
The Message, Eugene Peterson words it like this: "I
came so they can have real and eternal life, more
and better life than they ever dreamed of." The
King James Version says, "I am come that they
might have life, and that they might have it more
abundantly."

What is this full life, this better life, this abundant life? It has to be more than a reference to the
initial salvation experience. Many believers seem

to be searching for a more meaningful life even though they know that their sins are forgiven and they are on their way to heaven. They long for a deeper encounter with Jesus.

I believe that "life . . . to the full" is a reference to the Spirit-filled life. This concept is expressed in various ways. Some talk about being "totally committed" or "fully surrendered" to Christ. Others might refer to being "sanctified." Each of these distinctive terms points to a common Scripture. In Ephesians 5:18, speaking to believers, the Apostle Paul said, "Do not get drunk on wine, which leads to debauchery. Instead, be filled with the Spirit."

Paul would not have laid out this clear command for every believer if it were not essential for all of our lives. He emphatically states that this is an absolute necessity for entering a lifestyle of victory. Throughout the book of Acts, this was the one advantage the early church had over every enemy—they were endued with the power and boldness of a Spirit-filled life.

Some have said to me, "But brother Tom, I received all of the Holy Spirit when I was first converted!" I agree with anyone who would make this statement. However, just because we have all of Him does not mean that the Holy Spirit has all of us! Many of us come to Jesus for salvation out of a sense of fear, guilt and shame. We don't want to spend eternity in hell. So we confess our sins and invite Christ to become our Savior. But we can do all of that without giving ourselves totally to the Lord.

There is a deeper life for all Christians. It may or may not manifest itself in certain gifts of the Spirit, but this abundant life will always evidence itself in a display of the fruit of the Holy Spirit: "love, joy, peace, patience, kindness, goodness, faithfulness, gentleness and self-control" (Galatians 5:22-23). These become the character traits of the Spirit-filled believer.

Entering into Abundant Life

Like our salvation, the fully surrendered life must have a starting point which may begin shortly after conversion or years after we are saved. It is both a crisis and a process. It is a crisis in that it has a definite beginning; it is a process in that we must continue to be filled with the Spirit on a daily, moment-by-moment basis. Let's see what the Scriptures have to say.

1. Renounce self

In Romans 6:6-7, Paul said, "For we know that our old self was crucified with him so that the body of sin might be done away with, that we should no longer be slaves to sin—because anyone who has died has been freed from sin."

When Jesus Christ died on the cross, our old self, from which sin originates, died with Him. The apostle presents this as a completed act. Our rebellious self-life was rendered powerless through the death of the Savior. Theologically speaking, this is called "positional truth"—our position in Christ is freedom from the sin nature. It is a statement of fact. Practically speaking, this will not make a difference in our lives until we agree with God that this has really happened. Then and only then will the factual become actual in our experience.

This can also be referred to as "renouncing self." We must come to the place in our spiritual pilgrimage where we realize that sin is gaining the upper hand. "Now if I do what I do not want to do, it is no longer I who do it, but it is sin living in me that does it" (Romans 7:20).

We must come face to face with our inability to live a victorious Christian life in our own strength. We must repudiate all the efforts of the old nature to please God, because this just cannot happen. This is a life-changing realization which sooner or later dawns on every child of the kingdom: We must radically commit ourselves to the death of the old self.

Let me use an illustration of a strange funeral. I will pretend for a moment that a friend of mine has just died. At the funeral home, I walk up to the casket and whisper to my wife a juicy bit of gossip about the deceased. How would the corpse respond? Would he sit up and defend himself by saying, "Now hold on a minute here, Tom, that's just not true!" No, he wouldn't do this for one simple reason: He's dead. You can say anything you want to behind his back and he won't respond.

People can gossip about us, talk mean right to

our faces or even harm us physically. But we can be as calm and restrained as a dead person by the power of the Holy Spirit. We can count ourselves "dead to sin" (Romans 6:11).

I have witnessed this amazing energy in my own life. During difficult days in the pastorate, I have had to listen to many hurtful things said about me and my wife. I have read letters that were filled with anger and false accusations. Others have noted the calm serenity in my demeanor and asked how I could take this kind of abuse without striking back. Believe me when I say that it was not me—this was the Spirit of the living God who enabled me to respond in this Christlike manner.

We must agree with the Lord about the absolute truth of Romans 6:6: "For we know that our old self was crucified with him so that the body of sin might be done away with, that we should no longer be slaves to sin." On that basis we can renounce the old self with all of its sins—selfishness, self-centeredness, self-pity, self-indulgence, self-condemnation, etc. This leads to step two.

2. Receive the Spirit's fullness

> Now if we died with Christ, we believe that we will also live with him. . . . In the same way, count yourselves dead to sin but alive to God in Christ Jesus. (Romans 6:8, 11)

Just as we are saved by faith, we must receive the Spirit-filled life by simple trust in God's

Word. "We believe that we will also live with Him . . . alive to God in Christ Jesus." We go beyond mere death to self and accept the life of the Spirit in all its fullness. We can count on this like we can count on the sun rising tomorrow morning.

Many believers never get beyond the death of the old self to the abundant life in the Spirit. They may even talk about being dead to self, but in reality, they are just dead altogether!

3. Renewal day by day

The crisis aspect of Spirit-filled living is found in the renouncing of self and the reception of the Spirit's fullness, but the process of this abundant life is equally important. The best translation of the verb tenses used in Ephesians 5:18 and Romans 6:11 would look like this:

> "Do not get drunk on wine, which leads to debauchery. Instead, be always being filled with the Spirit."

> "In the same way, keep on counting yourselves dead to sin but alive to God in Christ Jesus."

Paul concludes his discussion of the fruit of the Spirit in Galatians 5 by saying:

> Against such things [the fruit of the Spirit] there is no law. Those who belong to Christ Jesus have crucified the sinful nature with its passions and desires. Since we live by the

Spirit, let us keep in step with the Spirit.
(5:23-25)

We begin to get the big picture. The "life . . . to
the full" is to be maintained on a daily, moment-
by-moment basis. We never really arrive at a spiritual level where it would not be necessary to abide
in Christ. Here are four suggestions for renewing
day by day.

First, we must have a *daily dealing with sin*. We
must keep short accounts with God and the people around us. We must not allow a few un-
checked sins to come together and form a wall.
We should strive to maintain a clear conscience,
dealing quickly and thoroughly with wickedness.

Second, we must experience a *daily death to self
and a fresh infilling of the Holy Spirit*. Even before
we roll out of bed, we need to recognize that our
old self no longer has dominion over us. We
should submit ourselves anew and afresh to the
control of the Spirit for that day, going throughout that day with the full awareness of His presence.

Third, we must have *daily devotions for strength*.
As I outlined in chapter 1, we must make time to
meditate on the Word and have two-way prayers.
This is not negotiable; it is not just for the super-
spiritual among us. Every Christian needs to have
time alone with the Lord every day.

Fourth, we need *daily direction for service*. We
must enter each new day with a sense that God is
leading and guiding us each step of the way, look-

ing for practical avenues of service. His plan becomes our plan. The day no longer belongs to us—it is totally His, and we will allow Jesus to direct us through it.

Have you come to the place in your spiritual life where you realize that you need to be filled with the Spirit in order to be a victorious Christian? Are you willing to renounce the old self, receive the Spirit's fullness and be committed to renewing this awareness each day?

The best response to the ten foolish things listed in this book is to do this one smart thing: Be filled with the Holy Spirit!

Finishing Well

I have fought the good fight, I have finished the race, I have kept the faith. Now there is in store for me the crown of righteousness, which the Lord, the righteous Judge, will award to me on that day—and not only to me, but also to all who have longed for his appearing. (2 Timothy 4:7-8)

Having received God's signal that he would soon be leaving this world, Paul offers his last will and testament. In three concise statements, he

149

summarizes his walk with Christ. It is the ultimate description of what it means to "finish well."

"I have fought the good fight." Paul acknowledges that it has been a struggle from the very start. The radical nature of his conversion in Acts chapter 9 provided several enemies for him from day one. Paul had been "hard pressed on every side . . . perplexed . . . persecuted . . . struck down . . ." (2 Corinthians 4:8-9).

But he was caught up in a "good fight." As I've described in chapter 5, some Christians are not in the real battle at all. They are focused on menial side issues that have nothing to do with the spread of the gospel. Paul was putting his energy into something eternal—something that really mattered.

"I have finished the race." Jesus said this of His own ministry as He hung on the cross: "It is finished" (John 19:30). Christ was referring to the completion of His mission among us and the provision for our redemption. In the same way, Paul was able to say with a clear conscience that his work for the Lord was done. A race is something that has a definite beginning and a precise ending, and the apostle was on his last lap, about to turn the corner on the home stretch.

"I have kept the faith." This cannot be said for every follower of Christ. Right after this testimony, Paul tells us that "Demas, because he loved this world, has deserted me and has gone to Thessalonica" (2 Timothy 4:10). In John 6:66, we read these sad words: "From this time many of his dis-

ciples turned back and no longer followed him."
And we are told that after the Savior was arrested,
His chosen disciples "deserted him and fled"
(Matthew 26:56).

It is a wonderful thing to be able to say with
Paul, "I have kept the faith." Perseverance is a rare
character quality in any generation. Once Paul
had made his complete commitment to Jesus
Christ, there was no turning back. He stood tall
through many difficult trials, even when they
were life-threatening.

The Apostle Paul finished well. He did not just
get a great start on the road to Damascus and then
slowly fade away. His candle grew stronger,
burned brighter and lasted longer as he progressed
in his spiritual journey. Paul's Christianity was
not like a pile of thorns which burned brightly but
briefly. Rather his pilgrimage was marked by
steady strides as he aspired to be Christlike. The
secret of this man's success is summed up in this
humble attitude:

> Not that I have already obtained all this,
> or have already been made perfect, but I
> press on to take hold of that for which
> Christ Jesus took hold of me. Brothers, I do
> not consider myself yet to have taken hold
> of it. But one thing I do: Forgetting what is
> behind and straining toward what is ahead, I
> press on toward the goal to win the prize for
> which God has called me heavenward in
> Christ Jesus. (Philippians 3:12-14)

Paul was also sustained by the realization that Jesus was ultimately responsible for keeping him. "I am not ashamed, because I know whom I have believed, and am convinced that he is able to guard what I have entrusted to him for that day" (2 Timothy 1:12).

His philosophy was very simple: Christ will safeguard any commitments we make to Him. We commit; He keeps. Paul knew that he could finish well because Jesus was the Guarantor. It is little wonder that Paul could look forward to the crowning day in glory when the King of all kings will give His rewards to His faithful servants. Paul was saying, as the songwriter said, "It will be worth it all when we see Jesus."

A Father and Mother Who Finished Well

As I am writing this, it has been nearly four years since my father died and two years since my mother passed away. It was a privilege to be raised by two godly parents, Bill and Madonna Allen. I am just one of their ten children, but the other nine would join me in saying that they both finished well.

My parents were both born in 1919. Though my father came from a good home, his parents, Earl and Cynthia, were very indifferent about spiritual things. During his college days in Indiana, my dad declared himself to be an atheist. For one of his psychology classes, he attended a revival service and had lots of fun mocking what he saw that night.

When my father graduated, he became a very successful insurance salesman and began to serve the god of materialism. He won several awards for his aggressive approach.

My mom's parents were devout Christians. Her mother pleaded with my dad to attend special evangelistic meetings. He finally agreed with the stipulation that she would promise to never bother him about religion again. She promised, and he went along for that opening service.

After he attended the first meeting, my father was so intrigued by what he heard that he decided on his own to come back the second night. (His mother-in-law almost fainted when she saw him come in!) After that second service, he made an appointment to see the visiting evangelist. They met the next day, and for several hours, Bill Allen, the cocky, successful insurance salesman, asked the preacher every imaginable question. And the evangelist's answers made a lot of sense.

As he left the office late that afternoon, my father said to himself, "I will either return to the service tonight and give my life to Christ, or I will burn every trace of religion in my home and never speak of it again!" Fortunately for me, he chose to do the former. The young atheist went forward on the very last verse of the invitational hymn and was dramatically born again.

The next day, he told his parents that he had been saved. His mother said, "What do you mean, Bill, were you in a car accident?" When he ex-

plained the spiritual transformation that had taken
place, they were totally stunned. As a result of his
zealous manner, he offended his parents by indi-
cating that they needed the forgiveness of Christ,
too, or they would spend eternity in hell. When
Cynthia began to cry, Earl ordered my dad out of
the house and told him to never come back again.

My father loved his dad very much, which
made his rejection extremely hard to take. He began to pray and fast one meal a week for the conversion of his mom and dad. Seven years after my
father's conversion, his parents prayed to receive
Christ as a result of his faithful life.

Not long after my dad's conversion, he felt a
strong desire to offer "eternal life insurance" to
people. He left the insurance business and followed God's call into the ministry. My mother
was somewhat reluctant, saying, "But I want a
nice house and a large family." Ironically, after my
father pastored four churches over forty-four
years of ministry, my mother got everything she
could have ever wanted.

Bill and Madonna Allen had ten children, all of
whom are walking with the Lord today. They
owned their own home and had a summer cabin
in Ontario, Canada. They traveled the world together sharing the good news of Jesus Christ.
Through many struggles and trials they remained
faithful.

Dad used to tell us about a three-week period of
spiritual depression that threatened to destroy his

life and ministry. It took place in the early years of his work for the Lord. He began to doubt his call to the ministry, the reality of the gospel and the very existence of God. He fasted, wept and prayed, but he could not seem to find the Lord.

What brought him out of this deep despair was a very simple truth that he never forgot: "You can praise your way through things you cannot even pray your way through." Jesus wanted my dad to praise Him even when he didn't feel like it. The Lord expected his unflinching commitment, even when he was struggling with doubts. After this experience, the rest of my dad's ministry was characterized by the joy of the Lord. It was hard to be around him without breaking into a smile.

Following the raising of ten children, my mother went back to school and finished her college degree. She became a schoolteacher and taught first grade for seventeen years in order to help her children get through college and graduate school. All ten kids are college graduates, and several of us have graduate degrees. We feel indebted to this wonderful woman who finished well.

My father's final pastorate lasted twenty-nine years. The church grew from 150 to 700 during that time, and five daughter churches were started from his congregation. Though he did not always share his heartaches with us, I know that he had times of great stress and strain. He even retired from the ministry on a good note because he knew when it was time to leave. Rather than hanging on for reasons of personal pride or insecurity, he left with his head held high while the saints offered a standing ovation. He finished well.

I had the privilege of speaking at both of my parents' funerals. Though we children were grief-stricken with the loss of these marvelous people, we were so grateful that they had both fought the good fight, finished the race and kept the faith. I am indeed thankful for this outstanding heritage. I know how special and beautiful it is when a believer finishes well.

As we observe Christians in the Church today, it is apparent that many of them will not finish well. The price seems to be too high to pay, but in actuality, it is much more costly the other way.

It is my prayer that the Lord will use this book to lead many into a Christian experience that will conclude with the doxology of Second Timothy 4:7-8. "I have fought the good fight, I have finished the race, I have kept the faith. Now there is in store for me the crown of righteousness, which the Lord, the righteous Judge, will award to me on that day—and not only to me, but also to all who have longed for his appearing."

As we leave behind the "Ten Foolish Things" cited here and embrace the Spirit-filled life, we too can know what it means to finish well.

*Ten Foolish Things Christians Do
to Stunt Their Growth*

Study Guide

by Tom Allen

Using This Study Guide

For Personal Study

Settle into your favorite chair with your Bible, a pen or pencil, a notebook and this book. Read a chapter at a time, marking portions that seem significant to you. Write in the margins, particularly noting those points that challenge you. Look up relevant Scripture passages. Then turn to the questions listed in this study guide. You can trace your progress by recording your answers, thoughts, feelings and questions in the notebook. Refer to the text of the book and the Scriptures as you allow the questions to enlarge your thinking. And pray. Ask God to give you a discerning mind for truth and a greater love for Himself.

For Group Study

Plan ahead. Before meeting with the group, read and mark the chapter as if you were preparing for personal study. Glance through the questions making mental notes of how you might contribute to your group's discussion. Bring a Bible along with this book to your meeting.

Offer an environment that promotes discussion. Comfortable chairs arranged in a casual circle invite people to talk with each other. It says, "We are here to listen, to respond to each other and to learn together." If you are the leader, simply be sure to sit where you can have eye contact with each person.

Involve as many as possible. Group learning works best if everyone can participate at some point. If you are a natural talker, pause before you enter the conversation. Then ask a quiet person what he or she thinks. If you are a natural listener, don't hesitate to jump into the discussion. Others can only benefit from your thoughts when you express them verbally. If you are the leader, be careful not to dominate the discussion. Help the group members to make their own discoveries.

Pace the study. The questions for each lesson are designed to last forty-five minutes to one hour. Early questions form the framework for later discussion, so don't rush by so quickly that you miss a valuable foundation. While the leader must take responsibility for timing the flow of questions, it is the job of each person in the group to assist in keeping the study moving at an even pace.

Pray for each other. Prayer should be offered during each lesson, but also make a commitment to remember others in prayer throughout the week.

Notice that each session includes the following features:

- *Lesson Topic:* a brief statement summarizing the lesson.

- *Fellowship Primer:* an activity or discussion to get acquainted with the lesson topic and/or with each other.

- *Key Questions:* a list of questions to encourage individual or group discovery and application.

- *Prayer Focus:* suggestions for turning one's learning into prayer.

- *Assignments:* assignments to complete prior to the next lesson.

Introduction: Overcrowded Nurseries

Lesson Topic

The reality of immaturity in the Church today.

Fellowship Primer

Break into groups of four to five people and have each person share a brief, perhaps humorous, personal illustration of something foolish he or she did and how it revealed an underlying immaturity. Take a lighthearted approach to this discussion time.

Key Questions

1. What are some of the implications of overcrowded "spiritual nurseries" in today's Church? How can we deal with them?

2. What forms of evidence did Paul offer to illustrate the immaturity of the Corinthian church (see 1 Corinthians 3:3)?

3. What are some illustrations of "jealousy, quarreling and carnality" in the modern

Church? How do these things mar our testimony and hinder our effectiveness?

4. How has our lack of suffering for Christ in today's Church become a roadblock to spiritual progress?

5. Discuss the examples of "foolish things" people did in the Old and New Testament times. What parallels do you see in your own life or in the Church in general?

6. Why is it important for us to be willing to admit that we have done foolish things? Where do we go from there?

Prayer Focus

• Quietly reread First Corinthians 3:1-4.

• Pray that while you study this book God will give you insight into those things that may be stunting your spiritual growth.

Assignments Prior to Lesson Two

1. Read through the "Ten Foolish Things" in the table of contents.

2. Read chapter 1, "A Mile Wide and an Inch Deep," while asking this question: Am I more concerned about my outward appearance or my inner heart?

Lesson 2

Chapter 1: A Mile Wide and an Inch Deep

Lesson Topic

Christians will not grow if they ignore their inner life with Christ and focus on outward appearance.

Fellowship Primer

Together as a group, have class members share TV, magazine or newspaper ads that demonstrate society's obsession with outward appearance.

Key Questions

1. Can you think of something you purchased that was beautiful on the outside but was actually defective on the inside? What was it?

2. Read the context surrounding the Lord's statement to Samuel in First Samuel 16:7. Why do you think that even a godly man like Samuel focused on the outward appearance?

3. What does it mean to live the Christian life "inside-out"? How can we do that?

4. In what ways do we focus on outward appearance? What are the consequences of this?

5. Have you experienced the "sponge" illustration recently? What came out of your life when you were squeezed by difficult circumstances?

6. Discuss the correlation between Psalm 42 and Philippians 3:10-11. Have you ever experienced the psalmist's longing for God? How can we cultivate this in our lives?

7. Why are devotional rituals harmful to going deeper with the Lord? How can we break out of these ruts?

8. Why must prayer be a "two-way street"?

Prayer Focus

• Ask God to forgive you if you have placed an emphasis on outward appearance instead of your inner life with Christ and accept His love and restoration.

• Pray that you will begin to live your Christian life "inside-out" and that you will get beyond ritualized daily devotions to the reality of living in the Master's presence moment by moment.

Assignments Prior to Lesson Three

1. Read through the "Ten Foolish Things" in the table of contents.

2. Read chapter 2, "The Lone Ranger Syndrome" while pondering this question: Have I begun to isolate myself from other believers? If so, why?

Lesson 3

Chapter 2: The Lone Ranger Syndrome

Lesson Topic

Christians will not grow in a vacuum—we need the Body of Christ.

Fellowship Primer

Have parents in various stages of parenthood share their experiences of watching their children in the quest for independence (as toddlers, teenagers and young adults). If there are no parents in the group, perhaps some older siblings can share or participants can tell stories of their own experiences of growing independent of their parents.

Key Questions

1. Is the desire for independence always wrong? What makes it become a sinful attitude?

2. Discuss the subtle process of the seduction of Adam and Eve (Genesis 3:1-19). How and by what things are we seduced in a similar way?

3. The author implies that disillusionment is part of the process of becoming a Lone Ranger Christian. How does a Christian become disillusioned? Have you ever felt this way? How did you deal with it?

4. How does Ephesians 2:11-12 complement First Corinthians 12:12, 18-20, 27?

5. Why is it vital to come to terms with the fantasy of the "perfect church"?

6. Why is encouragement important, especially in our world today? What are some practical ways we can "encourage one another daily"?

7. (For men only) Discuss the author's contention that men find it more difficult to share their feelings than women. How can men overcome this problem?

Prayer Focus

• Ask God to forgive you if a spirit of independence has gripped your heart and accept His love and restoration.

• Praise God for three specific things about the church you attend.

Assignments Prior to Lesson Four

1. Read through the "Ten Foolish Things" in the table of contents.

2. Read through chapter 3, "A Split Personality," and focus on this question: Am I developing both a sacred and a secular lifestyle?

Chapter 3: A Split Personality

Lesson Topic

If we are to avoid a "spiritually split" personality, we must integrate Christ into every aspect of our lives.

Fellowship Primer

Break into groups of four or five and discuss the temptation to become two different people because of the costly nature of following Jesus.

Key Questions

1. How do Jesus and James describe a "spiritually split" personality? (Luke 16:13 and James 1:8, 4:4)

2. Why are some Christians hesitant to demonstrate their spirituality around those who are unsaved? How do the social and secular personas reveal themselves in these situations?

3. Can you think of an example (no names, please!) of a person who is "suffering . . . as a

meddler" (1 Peter 4:15-16) rather than suffering for Christ?

4. What is "the mind of Christ"? How do we incorporate His mind into our daily lives?

5. Discuss the distinction between a "single tongue" and a "double tongue." How can we maintain a "single tongue"?

6. How are our behavior patterns affected by a "spiritually split" personality? How does this work against our spiritual maturity?

7. Read James 4:4. How does "friendship with the world" develop? How do we fight this danger?

8. (For parents only) How does your "spiritually split" personality affect your children?

Prayer Focus

• Ask God to forgive you if you have not integrated Christ into every aspect of your life and accept His love and restoration.

• Ask the Lord to give you courage to stand boldly for Him.

Assignments Prior to Lesson Five

1. Read through "Ten Foolish Things" in the table of contents.

2. Read chapter 4, "Bad Company," and consider these questions: Who/what is influencing my life the most, why is this so, and what effect is he/she/it having on my spiritual life?

Chapter 4: Bad Company

Lesson Topic

Outside influences can have a tremendous influence on our rate of spiritual growth.

Fellowship Primer

Together as a group, discuss influential people from your past—both positive and negative influences (teacher, athlete, neighborhood bully, best friend).

Key Questions

1. Why is it important to acknowledge the power of unholy alliances?

2. How do we deal with friends from our past? What should our relationships with them be like?

3. How can we achieve a sense of balance in our relationships with friends from our past?

4. What is "missionary dating"? Why is it dangerous ground?

5. Read Romans 12:18. What should we do about people who will not allow us to live at peace with them?

6. How can the advice of Susannah Wesley be applied to our lives today? How do we deal with things that are "morally neutral"?

7. What does Colossians 3:3 mean when it says we have died? How should that affect the way we live?

Prayer Focus

• Ask the Lord to forgive you and cleanse your heart and mind if you have allowed bad influences to take away your passion to be like Jesus and accept His love and restoration.

• Pray for daily discernment according to Philippians 4:8.

Assignments Prior to Lesson Six

1. Read through the "Ten Foolish Things" in the table of contents.

2. Read chapter 5, "Diversions," and ask yourself this question: What is preventing me from keeping the main thing the main thing in my walk with God?

Lesson 6

Chapter 5: Diversions

Lesson Topic

We must keep the main thing the main thing.

Fellowship Primer

Break into groups of four to five people and develop two lists: (1) a brief list of the things that really matter to God; and (2) a brief list of things that churches allow to become more important than they are in reality. Have each group share its lists.

Key Questions

1. What critical error did the coach of the Tigers make in preparing to play the Lions? (See chapter introduction.)

2. The author mentions some of Satan's greatest diversions. Can you think of others? Why do we get off track so easily?

3. Define the "organization diversion." Why is it not wise to directly transfer secular organizational theories over into the governance of the church?

4. How do we deal with nonessential doctrines? Is it possible to "agree to disagree"? Why or why not?

5. If political matters can become a diversion, should we then abandon all attempts to let our voices be heard as citizens of this country?

6. Is there a way to achieve balance in issues that can become diversions? If so, how?

Prayer Focus

- Ask God to forgive you if you have failed to remain focused on what really matters and accept His love and restoration.

- Pray that the Lord will renew your zeal for those things that are near and dear to His heart.

Assignments Prior to Lesson Seven

1. Read through the "Ten Foolish Things" in the table of contents.

2. Read chapter 6, "Dead Sea Disciples," while inquiring of yourself: Am I maintaining a balance between my spiritual intake and outlet?

Chapter 6: Dead Sea Disciples

Lesson Topic

The importance of keeping a balance between intake and outlet in the Christian life.

Fellowship Primer

Together as a group, discuss the issue of sleep. How much sleep does a person need? Is it the same amount for everyone? Can you get too much or too little sleep? Do you sleep better after an active day or a passive one? We need a balance between rest and work.

Key Questions

1. What principles for a growing Christian life can be gleaned from the Dead Sea?

2. Discuss the mission statement of Jesus and its implications for us (Matthew 20:28).

3. How does our environment as believers today lend itself to self-centeredness and depression?

How can we prevent this from happening?

4. What is so frightening about believers becoming bored and losing their focus? What are the consequences of this?

5. Is it true that the happiest parishioners are often the busiest? Why or why not?

6. The author calls the devil "the master of extremes." Is this an accurate observation? How common is extremism among Christians?

7. How does this chapter balance the truth of chapter 1?

8. Discuss the three benefits of servanthood.

Prayer Focus

• Ask God to forgive you if you have become a self-indulgent Christian and accept His love and restoration.

• Seek the Lord for that area of ministry where you can give to others and their needs.

Assignments Prior to Lesson Eight

1. Read through the "Ten Foolish Things" in the table of contents.

2. Read chapter 7, "Roller Coaster Religion," and ask yourself this: Am I living by faith or by feelings?

Lesson 8

Chapter 7: Roller Coaster Religion

Lesson Topic

We must learn to live by a steady faith rather than by our fickle feelings.

Fellowship Primer

Select two people to do a comedy sketch using the story in the introduction (the Christian Science practitioner and the man with the headache).

Key Questions

1. What are some examples of how we as a society are obsessed with how we feel? How do these examples affect our Christian growth?

2. What is the danger in basing our Christian experience largely on emotions? What can we do to balance our fluctuating emotions?

3. What can we learn about how Christ handled his emotions from Matthew 8:23-27? John 11:17-44?

4. Discuss the relevance of the "train" illustration. Does it describe your life? Why or why not?

5. What dangers could there be in a religious experience built largely around emotion?

6. How does Dr. A.B. Simpson's classic hymn, "Himself," assist our understanding of a Christian life built around faith?

7. How would you differentiate between happiness and joy? What is the place of each in the Christian life?

Prayer Focus

• Ask the Lord to forgive you if you have based your Christian experience around feelings.

• Ask the Lord to daily enable you to build your life around the faith in the facts of His Word.

Assignments Prior to Lesson Nine

1. Read through the "Ten Foolish Things" in the table of contents.

2. Read chapter 8, "Bitter or Better?" and ask this important question of yourself: Have I allowed the trials of my life to make me bitter or better?

Chapter 8: Bitter or Better?

Lesson Topic

The importance of allowing disappointment and tragedy to make us better rather than bitter.

Fellowship Primer

Break into groups of four or five people and have each person share an experience of disappointment or tragedy.

Key Questions

1. How is being a Christian easier or more difficult than being a nonbeliever?

2. Why is Christianity often unpopular? How do we deal with that?

3. Why do bad things happen to good Christians? Why must Romans 8:28 never be referred to out of the context of Romans 8:29?

4. How do we know that something good will result from trials? How does James 1:2-4 describe the good side of trials?

5. How have you dealt (or how are you dealing) with disappointments and tragedies? Have they made you bitter or better? Why or why not?

Prayer Focus

• Ask God to forgive you if you have become bitter through the trials of life and accept His love and restoration.

• Ask the Lord to show you how He is using disappointments and trials to make you more like Jesus.

Assignments Prior to Lesson Ten

1. Read through the "Ten Foolish Things" in the table of contents.

2. Read chapter 9, "The Sin That So Easily Entangles," and consider this question: Am I truly confronting sin in my life, or have I taken a passive approach to this matter?

Chapter 9: The Sin That So Easily Entangles

Lesson Topic

Believers must deal quickly and thoroughly with sin.

Fellowship Primer

Together as a group, discuss this question: What are the things that keep us from dealing with sin when it is present in our lives? (Make a list on a chalkboard or an overhead projector.)

Key Questions

1. Can you think of other examples like the DC-10 crash which illustrate how small things can make a huge difference?

2. Why is it so critical to call sin, sin? What happens when we fail to recognize sin for what it really is?

3. What are the three common sins? In what ways can you relate to them?

4. How can we differentiate between sins of omission and commission?

5. Why is it important to deal with each sin separately and within its own context?

6. What does it mean to repent? What are the implications and evidence of repentance in a person's life?

Prayer Focus

• Ask God to forgive you for any sins that have not been confessed and be willing to confess to others as is appropriate.

• Ask the Lord to enable you to deal daily with sin so you can maintain a clear conscience and continue growing.

Assignment Prior to Lesson Eleven

1. Read through the "Ten Foolish Things" in the table of contents.

2. Read chapter 10, "I Didn't Kill That Elephant!" and ask this question as you read: Have I really accepted the complete forgiveness of Jesus Christ for the sins I have confessed and forsaken?

Lesson 11

Chapter 10: "I Didn't Kill That Elephant!"

Lesson Focus

To be a victorious Christian, we must receive the unlimited grace and complete pardon for sin offered by the Savior.

Fellowship Primer

Together as a group, ask if anyone can think of an experience like the elephant story. (You thought you were guilty but found you were innocent.)

Key Questions

1. How does Christ deal with our sin when we repent? How does that affect the way you live?

2. Why is it essential to follow up the teaching of chapter 9 with the material here in chapter 10?

3. What is the importance of forgiveness—

both being forgiven and forgiving others? What does forgiveness show about your life?

4. Must we be able to understand how God can completely forgive us before we can enjoy the blessing of it?

5. How do you deal with past sin? How can our memory of past failure actually help us as we continue to confront sin in our lives?

6. What does it mean to have our sins cast to "the depths of the sea"?

Prayer Focus

- Ask God to reveal to you more of His unlimited grace and complete forgiveness.

- Ask the Lord to give you a forgiving heart toward those who have offended you.

Assignment Prior to Lesson Twelve

1. Read through the "Ten Foolish Things" in the table of contents.

2. Read chapter 11, "Life . . . to the Full," and ask yourself this: Am I experiencing the fullness of the Holy Spirit in my daily Christian life?

Chapter 11: "Life . . . to the Full"

Lesson Topic

The Spirit-filled life.

Fellowship Primer

Using a glass filled halfway with milk, ask the group, "What must I do to be able to say that this glass is full of water?" Answer: It must be completely emptied of the milk, cleaned and then filled with water. So it is in our lives if we would be filled with the Holy Spirit.

Key Questions

1. What does it mean to have "life . . . to the full"? How are we filled with the Holy Spirit?

2. What is the starting point or "crisis" that is needed before we can be filled with the Holy Spirit?

3. How does the cross make a difference in our

185

struggle with the old nature? How can we use that to our advantage?

4. What is the exchange of the old life for the Christ-life? What change should that bring about in our lives?

5. How can we receive the Spirit's fullness? How do we maintain the Spirit-filled life? Why is it a constant struggle?

Prayer Focus

• If you have not already done so, make a complete surrender of your life to Christ and ask Him to fill you with His Holy Spirit.

• Ask God to remind you daily of your need to be renewed by His Spirit.

Assignment Prior to Lesson Thirteen

1. Read through the "Ten Foolish Things" in the table of contents.

2. Read the epilogue, "Finishing Well," while inquiring: Am I living my life in such a way that I will finish well?

Lesson 13
_____

Epilogue: Finishing Well

Lesson Topic

Our goal should be to arrive at the finish line and hear Jesus say, "Well done. You've been a good and faithful servant!"

Fellowship Primer

Together as a group, talk about believers you have known who have already gone to glory having "finished well."

Key Questions

1. What does Second Timothy 4:7-8 tell us about what it means to finish well?

2. To which fight was Paul committed? Why are we fighting? What things do you personally fight against?

3. In what sense could Christ say, "It is finished" as He hung on the cross? In what sense could Paul say, "I have finished"? What did each mean? What was the secret of their success?

4. What are some examples of people in Scripture who did not keep the faith? What was their problem? Have you ever had similar problems?

5. What are some situations you have experienced that have helped you in your "fight"? How do those struggles give you an advantage now?

6. What changes do you need to make to ensure that you will finish well? How do we continue to "fight the good fight" without growing weary and giving in?

Prayer Focus

- Ask God to seal the truths of this book in your heart in such a way that you will continue to grow as a believer.

- Ask the Lord to develop the grace of perseverance in your life so that, along with Jesus and Paul, you can finish well.